My Two Wives and Three Husbands

S. Stanley Gordon

Savant Books and Publications
Honolulu, HI, USA

D1115077

Published in the USA by Savant Books and Publications
2630 Kapiolani Blvd #1601
Honolulu, HI 96826
http://www. savantbooksandpublications. com

Printed in the USA

Edited by Daniel S. Janik
Back Cover Photo by Penny Wolen, Photographer, All rights
reserved. Used with permission.
Cover Art and Design by Helen Babalis
Author Photo by Penny Wolen, Photographer, All rights reserved.
Used with permission.

13-digit ISBN:978-0-9829987-8-6
10-digit ISNB: 0-9829987-8-3

This work is a non-fictional memoir. Although the author has tried to
make the information as accurate as possible, the information comes
from memory. Many of the characters have died and it is not possible
to verify the accuracy of every statement included in the book. There
may be mistakes, both typographical and in content, and the
information conveyed is held to be current only up to the date that
the manuscript went into production. Therefore, this memoir should
be used only as an inspiration for further inquiry, not as an
authoritative informational source.

No person shall have any right to rely on the information contained
in this book, and neither the author, nor the editor, nor the publisher
shall be liable or responsible to any person or entity for any injury,
loss or damage caused, or alleged to have been caused, directly or
indirectly, by the information conveyed in this book.

Dedication

I dedicate this book to my immediate family: my son, Michael, my daughter-in-law, Rhoda, and my four wonderful grandchildren, Charles, Danielle, Ilana and Talia, all of whom have been loving and supportive, through thick, thin and in between.

My Two Wives and Three Husbands

PREFACE

Mae West, that icon of sexual liberty, gave me a line that I have used whenever people mention that I look younger than my eighty-some years and ask, "What's your secret?"

My reply: "I owe it all to dirty living!"

She meant, of course, unconventional living. Mae was always one to thumb her nose at society's puritanical mores, though always with humor. My kind of gal!

Looking back, I realize that I have crammed a lot into my years—much too much for just one book, so this one will focus on what I consider life's main attraction: LOVE. Business activities and earning money are important, of course, but at the end of the day they don't mean much if you can't share them with a lover who loves you back. That's what I stress to my grandkids today.

As I write these words, I am approaching my eighty-eighth birthday. At almost six feet tall, I am hale and hearty. When I look in the mirror, I see a face that could pass for sixty-five, while inside I feel thirty-four. Though my abundant head of hair has transitioned from jet black to salt-and-pepper to snowy white long ago, people tell me I am handsome. I have always considered it flattery, but lately I'm beginning to think it *might* just be true. I have lived a full and fulfilling life, encompassing several careers, and have few regrets. Although my tennis days are over, I occupy myself with theatre, travel, friends, and my loving spouse, of whom I will mention more—a lot more—later. Though my immediate family members live at some distance, we make sure to see each other frequently. Despite (or because of) some hard knocks over the years, I am happy to say that I'm still here, that life is even more full of wonder than ever before, and I am eager to see what life has in store for me in the future.

A word of caution at this point, however: If concepts like Hopeless Romantic, Love at First Sight or Head Over Heels make you nauseous, this book is definitely not for you. But if you have a zest for life's adventures and intrinsically understand that such clichés are never to be sneered at, then you're in for some wonderful fun, a few tears and, hopefully, some meaningful new insights.

YOUNG AND DIFFERENT

For many, childhood memories are like fragmentary, unrelated clips from a variety of movies—some important, others trivial. Psychology, however, says even the trivial are meaningful, like the tip of an iceberg signaling much, much more below the surface. That being said, some childhood memories are surprisingly intact.

My father, Pop, owned a small grocery store in Philadelphia, above which the family lived. In Russia, from which my parents emigrated after the turn of the 20th century, Jews were denied entry into the guilds of skilled workers and the professions; therefore, most Jews, like Pop, made a living in the new world as peddlers, merchants or storekeepers.

Our family name was Grodsky (my name-change

came later). A photograph of Pop—whose first name was Harry—and Mom—Sophie—taken when they had newly-arrived in Canada portrayed a handsome, somewhat stocky young man and a sturdy peasant girl. They were always vague about their ages when talking with the family, but in that picture they looked to me to be in their late teens or early twenties. My most vivid memories of them, of course, are of a middle-aged and, later, elderly couple.

They arrived in Halifax, Nova Scotia, around 1905 and settled in Montreal where Harry's older brother, Israel, had already emigrated with his wife. A few years later my parents moved to Philadelphia, Pennsylvania, USA, where another brother, Benjamin, had arrived and settled with his wife.

It never occurred to me to query my parents about their lives in Canada or Russia. By the time I wished I had, it was too late. The truth is that I was ashamed of their foreignness: their heavy accents and peasant manners. I wanted to be "American." They embarrassed me. Now I feel more ashamed of myself. Oh, to be able to re-live the past!

Between 1905 and 1916, Mom gave birth to three

sons and one daughter and thought that her childbearing days were over. But six years later, I came along. She fervently hoped for another girl, but I was what she got. Undismayed, she lavished attention and affection on me, and I reciprocated, loudly proclaiming, at the age of five or six, "When I grow up I'm going to marry my mother," as Mom beamed proudly. After all, it seemed to me that love led to marriage, and I loved Mom dearly, so what could be more natural?

The Pop I knew was a passive man, already beaten down by life. I never saw him angry; he seemed resigned to accepting what fate laid down for him. Mom, on the other hand, never stopped complaining. Even when something was good, it could have been better.

Pop readily acquiesced to the demands of his nagging wife, though as a child, I was oblivious to such distinctions. After Pop retired, late in life, the worm turned with a vengeance. I recall his interrupting Mom one day and exclaiming, in an unusually loud voice, "Woman, SHUT UP!"

I'll never forget the wounded look on Mom's face as she turned to me and said, "You see? You hear the way he talks to me?" I had to turn away to hide the grin on my face.

Pop labored in the store from 7 a.m. to 9 p.m., six days a week, never sitting down to a real meal, instead grabbing bites between customers at slack times. Besides being a fast eater, he was an early riser.

It was still dark one morning when, at grammar-school age, I sleepily climbed out of bed and toddled down the hall to the bathroom. As I passed my parents' bedroom, I could hear my father getting dressed to go downstairs and open the store. He was muttering something to himself and I paused to listen. What I heard was a big sigh and then, "What a shitty life."

Why doesn't he change his life? I thought. But even to this child, the answer was obvious: He hadn't the tools to better himself and was trapped by the need to provide for his family. I determinedly resolved that, if my life ever turned "shitty" like that, I would change it. I would take action. At least, I would do *something!*

Another early memory was of playing a game with a neighbor's kid on his porch. We were about eight and it was Sunday, when Philadelphia's Blue Laws demanded that all stores be closed, including my father's corner grocery. It was summer. The windows were open—in the late 1920's no one had air-conditioning—and we overheard my chum's mother telling her husband she had forgotten to buy sliced meat for sandwiches that day.

Playing the hero, I said to my friend, "I'll get my father to open the store for her," and he rushed inside to give his parents the good news. A moment later, through the open window, I heard his father's reply: "Tell that Goddamn Jew to go scratch his ass!" I was stunned. It felt like someone had slapped me. Out came my friend, who stopped short when he saw my face. "What's the matter?" he asked. "You look like you're going to cry." I mumbled something to the effect that I needed to go home, and fled. I was to quickly learn that, to some, the word was not "Jew" but "Goddamn Jew."

My father's small grocery stores—he had several in succession—were always located in gentile working-class neighborhoods, where anti-Semitism was often not only rampant but also outspoken. When I was old enough to play street games with the local boys, invariably someone would make a crack about the "kikes" or the "Goddamn Jews," only to realize suddenly that one was in their midst. "Oh," the person would say, "I didn't mean you…you're different!" to which I wanted to shout, "I am NOT different…you don't *know* any other Jews!" But, of course, I didn't. Instead, I learned to adopt an exterior of stony indifference. Mustn't let them see I can be hurt. That outer shell was to come in handy later, when I had to hide my other big "difference."

A persistent memory I have is that of being a passenger in a car being driven by an older friend—I was about ten years old then. A second schoolmate was also present. We were driving by the school we both attended when my school chum mentioned that two of our male teachers were getting married the following week. "To each other?" I inquired. "Of course not, silly!" the driver replied. "Men can't marry each other!" to which I innocently asked, "Why not?" The reply came back, "Because they can't, that's all." Which seemed to me to be no answer at all. To this day, I have never heard a satisfactory answer to that question. Why not, indeed?

My oldest brother, Ben, was a good-natured, affable, out-going guy who followed in Pop's footsteps. Ben was an ideal older brother—benevolent, with an always-ready smile on his good-looking face. He was the tallest of us with a build most would call lanky. Easy-going, Ben had no ambition to be anything other than a store-keeper like Pop, and, sure enough, he eventually owned his own delicatessen in a working-class gentile neighborhood, which he operated with the help of an adoring wife. Ben did not turn into Pop, I'm happy to say, but retained his sunny outlook throughout his life. I can still see that broad grin as he greeted every friend with, "Hey, man! How ya doin'?"

Two years younger than Ben, my sister, Anna, was good-hearted, well-meaning and loving. However, she was a *girl*, which placed her in a somewhat remote and mysterious place to me. An unfortunate childhood accident left Anna with a slight limp. Otherwise, she was attractive and even shapely. She had no dearth of male suitors, settling on one quite early. And that limp never got in the way of her enjoying a dance floor. She also had a beautiful singing voice, as did I at a young age, and we sometimes regaled family and guests with duets.

Next came Meyer, who was my hero: he was smart, ambitious and very good-looking. In me, Meyer saw some of the same abilities he had, and took me under his wing, becoming the father my real one had no time to be. Of course, I looked up to him! More truthfully, I had a "crush" on him. And why not? Although a little shorter than I, Meyer was dapper, with movie-star looks and charisma. Plus he had brains. Working part-time throughout college, his ambitions took him to a position as a Professor of Physics at a university, then on to becoming an independent building contractor. Meyer really cared about me, and was determined that, like him, I would get a college education. He married a wonderful girl who loved him deeply and who became a good friend to me later, when fate dealt Meyer a terrible blow. Like Ben, he was usually smiling, but with a mischievous gleam in his eye that suggested deep channels within.

Next came Dave, six years older than I. We shared a twin-bedded room. A memory clip I have from back then is of staring at the bare skin on his arms as he lay sleeping, while I experienced something new that I couldn't fathom at the time. Later, I learned it was arousal. Dave and I were never close, however; our personalities were too disparate. Looking back, I feel sorry for Dave. When the genes were dispersed, he got shortchanged. Instead of his siblings' sunny dispositions, Dave was always on edge, with occasional outbursts of temper. He wasn't bad-looking, but his dour disposition gave him a tight, nervous appearance. Oddly enough (or perhaps not so oddly) he married a woman much like himself and their married life was a constant battle. I often wondered why they didn't divorce or separate, until it occurred to me that they enjoyed the conflict. Some people are only happy when they are unhappy! Through the years, although we tried to act like brothers, the feeling simply wasn't there. A shame, but I guess it happens in the best of families.

With puberty came masturbation and, despite all of the many images of shapely women that appeared everywhere in ads, movies and magazines, the image in my mind during the act was of a male bodybuilder— Charles Atlas—kneeling and holding a globe of the world on his back, in ads in several magazines.

That should have been a clue, but in those days the subject of homosexuality was strictly taboo. I had never heard the word. I knew something was awry when seeing a live girl in a bathing suit elicited no special response from me, whereas seeing even a photo of a half-naked man left me with butterflies in my stomach and weak knees. So I faced the fact that I was sexually attracted to men instead of to women. I was a freak! Surely I was the only person in the world who felt that way!

This is my unique destiny, my Achilles' heel, I thought. *What a rotten trick God was playing on me! It must forever remain a dark secret, never to be revealed to anyone.*

11

Then one day, I read in a movie gossip magazine the shocking news that a famous male actor had been arrested for "homosexuality"—actually, it said he had solicited sex from an undercover male detective. *Wow!* I thought. *There* are *others besides me, and they live in Hollywood! I'll have to somehow go there one day. But even then, no one must ever find out about my secret desires or I'll be arrested and thrown into jail.*

My very next action was a trip to the public library to look up "that word." What I discovered was a scientific treatise by Havelock-Ellis that proclaimed homosexuality to be a perversion, and one after another medical tomes that called it an aberration akin to a disease. This was definitely not good!

Delving further, I found a work of fiction on the subject entitled "The Well of Loneliness," written by a lesbian—another new word—and I hastened to read the book. My situation became even worse: The heroine ended up killing herself in despair because of "the love that dares not speak its name."

Of course, I had other problems as well: All through grammar school and part of high school, I struggled with stammering....even stuttering at times. It's said today that this problem is a result of unresolved inner stress, which I certainly had. But I made a dramatic recovery when, one day, one of my teachers said to me, "I saw you in the class play recently, and you didn't stammer at all. Why is that?" That got me thinking, and I realized that, while acting, I was concentrating on the *effect* of each phrase, rather than on what I wanted to say, so I decided to carry that technique over into my everyday life. It worked! For a while, I only stammered when my mind ran ahead of my mouth; soon I rarely stammered at all.

Another problem: Teen angst. In junior high and high school, everyone travelled in cliques. They all seemed self-confident and high-spirited, while inside I felt inferior, ashamed, and desperately afraid of being found out. I made a big effort to be "with it," and participated in numerous after-school social activities. Basically shy and fearful, I put on a good front. Being poor, Jewish and a closeted homosexual certainly increased my frustration.

Luckily, I was a good student receiving top grades, which helped me get accepted by some groups...and ostracized by others! I tried hard to compensate and, by my senior year, had become editor of the school newspaper. I was even elected as an officer of the graduating class. In actuality, I was honing my acting skills. So far so good!

At this age, the sexual juices were raging, and two of my classmates decided it was time for the three of us to lose our virginity. One fellow knew of a prostitute whose fee was within our meager budgets. I was severely in doubt about my ability to perform with a woman, but how could I say "No" without revealing my secret? So, off we went.

Hers was a one-woman, private business in her small apartment, and one of us went into her bedroom while the other two waited in an anteroom. I insisted on being last. When it was my turn, the woman, who seemed middle-aged to me (though she was probably in her thirties), was in the process of cleansing herself as I entered. She was wearing a dress but apparently nothing underneath. The only thing I remember about her appearance was that she was plain-looking—not pretty, not ugly, just plain.

When she saw me, she laid down on the bed, pulled up her dress and said, "Okay, come on."

I unzipped my fly, took out my flaccid penis and dutifully climbed aboard. Nothing! "Oh God," she muttered, trying to finger life into my lifeless member, adding, "I hate having to deal with a cherry." After more than a few minutes of no results, we gave up and, mortified, I paid her the agreed-upon price.

Emerging into the other room where my two friends were waiting, I, of course, proudly boasted about the terrific experience, just as they had, and we left. Afterward, I wondered if, indeed, they had both really "scored." Probably so, I decided. Well, anyway my secret was still intact—along with my virginity!

In my junior and senior years of high school, I started dating girls. It was the thing to do. Otherwise, friends and schoolmates might consider me strange, retarded or "queer" (by now queers had become an object of derision and snickers). Although there was no way I could prevent someone from calling me a "Goddamn Jew," I'd be damned if I would provide anyone with a reason to call me a "Goddamn Queer" behind my back!

While the jocks were bragging about "making out" with this or that girl, I maintained the fiction that "a gentleman never tells" and hoped I'd get by with that. Necking was compulsory, of course, so I kissed all of my dates, but it was perfunctory, at least on my part, and I was careful not to date the same girl more than a few times. It may have given me the reputation of being a fickle Lothario, but the truth was, my sexual fantasies continued to be about men.

High school graduation, scheduled for June of 1940, was fast approaching. The University of Pennsylvania and Temple University each awarded a full scholarship to the number one and number two graduates, respectively, at my high school. I had always been in the top two, so I was confident of getting one, which would finally resolve the problem of being from a poor family. For whatever reason, however, Temple University did not give any scholarship that year, and I graduated number two, losing to a girl, no less! While pondering my options, a letter arrived out of the blue to decide my first career path.

One of the last girls I dated before graduation, Lillian, had a brother who practiced optometry in Philadelphia. Unbeknownst to me, they had submitted my name and credentials to the local Pennsylvania State College of Optometry—not related to Penn State University—for a scholarship to its four-year doctorate program. In the envelope was a letter offering me the scholarship. So that, at last, settled that.

I rewarded Lillian by subsequently dropping her. Oh, callow youth! Well, I rationalized, I did her a favor by not letting her get involved with someone who could never love her the way she would want to be loved. And it was true, though I still feel guilty every time I think about it (if you read this, Lillian, I hope you will forgive me).

So now I was a freshman in college. Busy, busy, busy. Too busy to worry about my continually growing inclination, until one day I happened to read a personal ad in a local newspaper—to this day, I cannot recall why, since it was not my habit. The ad was from a gentleman seeking to meet a young man for "stimulating conversation." Well, my inner voice told me what that meant, so I lost no time in calling the phone number. He invited me to visit him at his downtown apartment for tea. *Tea?* I thought. *Ha!*

To my surprise, he served tea...and biscuits! He was the perfect middle-age gentleman. We sat quietly and chatted and, as I thought it would, the conversation eventually veered to the subject of homosexuality. He voiced contempt for the "common queers" who frequented downtown Philadelphia's Rittenhouse Square each night. My ears perked up...they were here, nearby! No need to go to Hollywood! I could hardly wait to take my leave. He, very prim and proper, didn't even ask for my phone number. Instead, he asked me to call soon for another date, if I liked, but I never did.

The very next night found me seated on a bench in Rittenhouse Square. By day, the small park was a green oasis flanked by posh apartments and fancy hotels. It was frequented by nannies pushing baby carriages, and filled with elderly couples walking or sitting sedately. But at night, it transformed into another world altogether.

Men of various ages and descriptions leisurely strolled around the park's inner ring; other men, much like myself, were sitting on benches. As one walked by another, their eyes would meet and, if there was attraction, the glance would turn into an intense stare and the pickup rite would begin.

I was beside myself with nervous excitement! It wasn't long before an attractive young man walking by caught my eye. He paused as I stared at him. I found out later that the usual approach was to ask for a light, even if no cigarette was in sight, but this fellow was more direct. "Are you alone?" he asked.

"Yes," I managed to squeak out.

"Do you mind if I sit?"

"Not at all." I managed to keep the quavering out of my voice.

He sat. Silence. Then, "Are you a student?"

"Yes, I'm a freshman in college. What about you?" I was feeling bolder.

"I'm a church organist," he declared.

More small talk ensued as we gingerly beat around the bush. Then he inquired, "Do you live around here?"

"No," I said, adding, "I live in North Philadelphia… with my parents. What about you?"

"I live alone," he answered. "I have an apartment just two blocks from here." A few minutes of silence later he popped the question: "Would you like to come by for a drink?"

I feigned nonchalance. "Okay," I acquiesced and off we went. We never got to the drink, which was just as well for all the butterflies that had invaded my stomach.

No flaccidity that night! It was all of my fantasies come true, and neither of us did much sleeping the entire night. I had thoughtfully prepared my family for the possibility of my staying overnight with a school chum on weekends, and tonight was Saturday night, so they wouldn't worry, and I could catch up on sleep the next day. But who needed sleep? I was overjoyed, excited, exhilarated—eager to repeat the experience.

From the intense level of that evening's activities, my

organist friend no doubt assumed that we would go on seeing each other, but I put an immediate end to that expectation. "This is a whole new world for me," I explained, "and I want to experiment with other people." He was crestfallen but accepted it with visible sorrow. I felt no guilt. If I was to maintain a secret inner life, separate from my outer life, there was no way I could enter into a real relationship, with phone calls and letters and candle-lit dinners and emotional involvement. No way!

A funny thing happened at about this time: Paul, a fellow high school graduate with whom I maintained contact, had gone to Georgia to spend a few weeks with friends. I had received a postcard from him, and replied with what I thought was an innocuous remark about watching out for those Southern belles. Little did I know that "belle" was one of many secret code words that meant a gay man.

Paul was now back in town and called, suggesting we see a movie together, which we did. Afterward, we went to his home for a late snack and he proceeded to grope me. As I recoiled in surprise, he asked what was wrong. "How could you know if this would be okay with me?" I stammered.

"I knew from your postcard," he replied. After he explained, we had a wonderful laugh about my unintentional gaffe.

Later that evening, he informed me that another graduate named Sid, whom I knew quite well—or thought I had—was also gay. The three of us became buddies...or rather "sisters," which was the term for gay friends who do not have sex with each other.

They taught me a lot about this new world I was discovering, and a whole new world it was! It was a secret, underground world with its own language. Words like "gay," "cruising," "swishy," "campy" had not yet been usurped by straights.

There were clandestine meeting places—gay bars and bathhouses—where gay men could meet. It amused me no end that the downtown bathhouse that turned gay every evening also happened to be the very same bathhouse where my mother met her lady friends for their weekly afternoon shvitz bath (schvitz is Yiddish for "sweat"). I couldn't work up the nerve to go to a bathhouse, but the three of us did go to a downtown gay bar.

I'll never forget my first night at that bar. As we

approached the door, I hesitated, my heart in my mouth. I was actually trembling—whether from excitement, or anxiety, or fear of not knowing what to expect, or how to behave, I'll never know—but in we went. I had only recently turned eighteen, the legal age for drinking, and Paul and Sid were the same age. Most of the bar patrons were older men. We were new faces so, naturally, much attention was bestowed upon us.

This was not at all like picking up someone at Rittenhouse Square. This required blatant social interaction, and it threw me for a loop. Paul and Sid, having been there before, could see I was feeling inadequate and insecure, so they didn't mind when I suggested we leave after a brief interval.

The following week, however, we went back, and this time, my nervousness having subsided, I felt more at ease and engaged in friendly banter with some of the denizens. By my third visit I was totally self-confident, and didn't hesitate in saying "Yes!" to an attractive man who invited me to have a drink at his apartment. Of course, the drink segued into sex. One-night-stands became my new credo.

Not long after our third visit to the gay bar, Paul's

mother came across a love letter written to Paul by one of his suitors. Confronting him angrily, she demanded that he seek treatment. When he defiantly refused, his parents cast him out of the house. Undaunted, he moved to Manhattan, where he got a job and later, I learned, opened a fancy gift shop on Madison Avenue. I say, "I learned," because, for some reason, he dropped his Philadelphia friends, and we lost contact. Sid's friendship, on the other hand, remained constant and was to benefit me in later years.

After Judy Garland appeared as Dorothy in "The Wizard of Oz," we gays referred to ourselves as "friends of Dorothy" ("Toto, I have a feeling we're not in Kansas anymore!"). During World War II, military intelligence, trying to ferret out gays, had a devil of a time trying to track down this "Dorothy" who seemed to have so many conspiratorial friends!

About the same time, Danny Kaye, in his hit Broadway musical of 1942, "Let's Face It," sang: "Don't inquire of Georgie Raft, Why his cow has never calfed; Georgie's bull is beautiful, But he's GAY!"

It went over the heads of most of the audience, but we in the know smirked and giggled. Nudge, nudge, wink, wink!

There was a delicious edge to being part of this secret fraternity that existed right under the noses of the "squares." The fact that we were doing something that polite society regarded as illicit simply added to the spice. As my favorite philosopher and queen of innuendo, Mae West, said, "To err is human…and it's *so* divine!"

It did, however, entail learning to live a double life, and while I slowly assumed the role, I had to be constantly on guard. I was still dating girls, though chastely. Some weekends, I was busy with college or family functions, but most Saturday nights found me seeking—and often finding—liaisons with gay men. Looking back on it, those first few years of college were filled with periodic debauchery. Let's face it: I was a teen-age slut!

Then something started to shift inside: I was approaching twenty and exiting my teens. Maybe it was maturation, or maybe the gay scene was becoming so familiar as to start having a numbing effect. Whatever, I began to feel something was missing. The fun was palling; I felt a void inside. I was in a quandary, confused, at odds with myself.

And then I met Irene.

IRENE

It was 1942, and America was at war. After Pearl Harbor, I hastened with my classmates to enlist and serve my country in its time of need. Instead, being within two years of graduating from a professional school, I was given a student deferment. After two years, if the war was still going, I would enter boot camp as a cadet, to become an officer in the Army Air Corps (in those days, each branch of the armed services had its own air corps; it was only after the war that they were consolidated into one Air Force).

The where and how of my meeting Irene is still hazy; I know we began dating, as I had with countless other girls, but something sparked between us. Maybe she came along at just the right moment, or maybe there was something special about her—more likely both, now that

I think back on it. After a few months, when I would customarily switch to a new woman, I found myself wanting to continue seeing her.

Irene was pretty, down-to-earth, fun and comfortable to be with. Her demeanor was always pleasant. Our personalities and outlooks were similar. She was truly a "sweet"-heart.

Irene came from a middle-class Jewish family, the youngest of three daughters, with parents who were the opposite of mine: Her father was domineering and forceful...he could be a bully on occasion, while Irene's mother was pleasantly subservient.

No butterflies in my stomach or weak knees, but I nonetheless developed a genuine affection for her, and—wonder of wonders—necking with Irene gave me an erection. Wow! My gay world suddenly turned topsy-turvy. Could it be that all I needed was the right girl? Was the house with the picket fence and the kids and the PTA a possibility after all? It boggled my mind and soon I resolved to spend most of my Saturday nights with her.

Necking led to petting, but since a nice Jewish boy in those days simply did not go "all the way" with a nice Jewish girl, I didn't. But I wanted to, and that was the

26

important thing for me! I didn't totally abandon my gay encounters, but they gradually slackened off and eventually slid away, and I decided that maybe it had all been merely adolescent shenanigans. Perhaps it was time to "put away childish things." Then, out of the blue came orders to report to boot camp three weeks hence. I was completely taken by surprise. Graduation day was still six months away, and with the war still raging, there was no appeal. Several other students found themselves in the same situation, so the college agreed to grant us our diplomas in absentia. Off I went, after genuinely tearful goodbyes with family and Irene.

It was wintertime, and boot camp was high in the blustery, cold mountains of North Carolina, and it was men, men, men—young men—all around me, 24/7! What a test for my new resolve! The army kept us busy from pre-dawn to late-night, but I soon noticed an adorable, quietly introverted and gently appealing lad in the cot next to mine. Still I kept my resolve. Besides my genuine commitment to Irene, I couldn't risk being unmasked and disgraced with a dishonorable discharge. So instead, I wrote affectionate letters to Irene and she to me.

I did, however, slip once. A bout with psoriasis sent me to the military hospital in Asheville, North Carolina, where I was treated as an outpatient for a few weeks. This meant finding temporary lodgings in town and having lots of free time on my hands. I quickly found myself "cruising," and equally quickly being "cruised" back by an attractive young civilian man. We saw each other several times during my stay in Asheville. I told myself it was just because I felt so lonely, reasoning that I wasn't really cheating on Irene, since I wasn't bedding another woman. It was easy to find an excuse for doing what I wanted to do, even knowing I shouldn't.

The boot camp ordeal finally came to an end, and I was sent to Yale University for actual officer training. The rigorous schedule of boot camp proved nothing compared to the demands of this new regime. Literally every single moment was accounted for and crammed with supervised activity, so any hanky-panky was impossible. On Sundays—our only off-duty day—I either took the train to Philadelphia or Irene trained up to New Haven for the day. And so it went until I received my commission as a lieutenant. The military powers that be weren't quite sure what an optometrist was—other than it somehow involved optics—so, naturally, they assigned me to teach bombardiers how to use the new, ultra-secret

Norden bombsight at Boca Raton, Florida. But first, they granted me a few weeks leave and, during that interval, Irene and I were married.

Our marriage ceremony was a full-dress affair at a fancy downtown Philadelphia hotel, with Irene in white, me in my lieutenant uniform, both of our families plus assorted friends in attendance. The whole enchilada! Or, rather, the entire matzo ball! At the traditional breaking-of-the-wineglass moment in the ceremony, it took me two attempts to accomplish the demolition...a bad omen which everyone pretended to ignore, though I remember hearing muttering in the background.

Off we went by train to honeymoon in Miami for a week. That very day happened to be D-Day, when the Allies crossed the English Channel to invade Nazi-occupied France, so the next day, this smart-ass post-carded his friends with the message, "Both invasions going well" (cringe). It happened to be true, so I was much relieved. Phew!

After our honeymoon, duty down in Boca Raton became more like working in a luxurious resort. Irene and I found a cute little house in Fort Lauderdale, which we shared with another newly-married couple. Life was pleasant and uneventful, and if I cast a few longing glances at the hoards of attractive young men, it was no big deal.

After about a year, I was transferred to teach at Victorville, California. There, we boarded with a local family. By this time, my longings to "sleep" with a man were gaining in strength, and it was taking much more conscious effort to suppress them. Still, I did.

Irene worked as secretary to the Commandant of the Army Air Corps Base in Victorville. One day, she was typing up orders for men to be shipped to the South Pacific—victory had finally been secured in Europe—when she came across my name. Marching into her boss's office, she declared, "You've got my husband's name on this list to be shipped out!"

"So?" he said.

"So if he ships out," she responded, "then I go back to Philadelphia, and you'll have to break in a new secretary."

After thinking things over for a moment, he said, "Scratch his name off the list." So thanks to Irene, I never saw action in the bitter Pacific war!

When Japan finally surrendered and World War II officially ended, Irene went back home while I went to

Marysville, California, to be discharged. Thankfully, I wasn't there long enough to get into any trouble, and joined Irene in Philadelphia a short time later to ponder our options.

We were staying with Irene's parents at the time, and I decided to take the Pennsylvania State Board of Optometry exams, which were being given a few months hence, in case we decided to stay in Philadelphia. To prepare, I re-enrolled in my *alma mater* and took some refresher courses. It was in one of those classes that I met Martin Kanter, who was to become a lifelong friend.

Marty was single, smart, sincere, friendly...and straight. We hit it off immediately. We studied together, and soon he met Irene and the three of us began socializing together.

My struggles to suppress my homosexual feelings during this time were becoming more difficult, and I felt a powerful need to confide in someone. Somehow, I felt sure I was safe in choosing Marty, so I told him about my situation while we were alone one day. I was right. At first, he was somewhat nonplussed, but he quickly recovered and proceeded to do what he felt a male best friend should do: urge me to see a psychiatrist.

Marty actually took me to the doctor's office and sat

in the waiting room while I had my session. I have completely blocked any memory of what transpired during those fifty minutes, but I never went back. Still, it felt good to know that I had a friend who knew my secret and was supportive. As a matter of fact, he was the only single, straight man I ever felt truly close to. I felt I could confide anything to him and he would honor my confidence without judging me. That's a true friend, in my book.

I passed the Pennsylvania Licensing Board Exams, but in the meantime Irene and I decided to move to California and settle in Los Angeles, where I had distant relatives whom we had met before, and liked. Looking back, I wonder if there was also a subconscious pull from my early knowledge of gays in Hollywood.

We took an apartment in an old but respectable part of East Hollywood. Irene found a job as a secretary, and I prepared for the California Licensing Board Exams, which would allow me to practice optometry in California. I passed the written tests easily, but flunked the oral portion, receiving no explanation or appeal. I reasoned that this was how they kept a lid on the large numbers of professional graduates who wanted to move to California at the time. While waiting to re-take the state board exams six months later, I took a part-time job selling outdoor furniture at the May Company, a local department store, while taking post-graduate courses at a local optometry college.

One day, actress Jessica Tandy was browsing in the furniture department at the May Company. I knew of her big success on Broadway as Blanche DuBois in "A Streetcar Named Desire," opposite Marlon Brando. I had also read of how Twentieth Century Fox had signed her to a contract and had brought her to Hollywood. And there she was, my first star encounter, just a few feet away!

After the customary, "Can I help you?" I managed to engage her in conversation, during which I mentioned how pleased Darryl Zanuck must be to have her at his studio. To which she succinctly replied, "Darryl Zanuck? He wouldn't know who I was if he fell over me!" That was my first lesson in show business a-la-Hollywood.

Reasoning that it might put me in good stead with the State Board of Optometry, I also volunteered to be a clinic chief, supervising senior students as they practiced their profession on indigent patients. Whether or not it helped, this time I passed and received my California license.

Now that I was contemplating beginning my professional life, I wanted to change my name. My family name was Grodsky. Somehow, somewhere, much later, I picked up an interesting story about the family name. It went something like this: As a small boy, my great-grandfather was swept up by Cossacks off the streets of his village in Russia. It was one way they obtained recruits. He was raised as a Cossack; all his family memories were erased. When he was old enough to realize what had happened, he deserted the Cossacks and emigrated to the nearest large city, Kiev.

Not knowing his real family name, he chose a name meaning "Son of the City." In Russian, "grad" means "city," while "sky" means "son of," so he adopted the name Gradsky. In the new world, immigration authorities heard it as Grodsky. None of my then-living siblings knew anything about this account, so there is doubt as to its authenticity. I know I didn't make the story up, but could I have possibly dreamed it? Anyway, it was a colorful story. I liked it and wanted to believe it, so that was enough for me.

My first name was Samuel, a distinctly Jewish name.

Together, my first and last name signified "foreign Jew." At the time, however, it wasn't so much the foreignness and Jewishness that were paramount in my conscious thoughts, but that I wanted the name on my shingle I was about to hang out to be one that would be easily remembered by the average American.

That's when I hit upon the last name "Gordon," which *could* be Jewish, contained many of the same letters, and was common yet singular enough to be remembered. At the same time, I adopted the middle name "Stanley" for no reason except that I preferred it to Samuel. I now know that I was subconsciously justifying selecting Stanley to use in my "secret" life.

While I was changing names, I thought I might as well make another change I had been contemplating for some time. That was to fix my nose. It had a small hump that loomed large in my mind, so I had the hump removed. It didn't change my appearance appreciably, but it lifted my self-confidence, so I viewed it then and now as worth the trouble and expense. Ah, vanity!

Meanwhile, Irene and I re-contacted my cousins who lived in the area; we were also rapidly making new friends and becoming caught up in the social whirl of middle-class Hollywood. Added to that, there was the anticipation of opening my own office in the near future.

Underneath it all, my homosexual proclivities were also bubbling. I thought about men. I dreamed about men. Eventually, in order to have sex with Irene, I began imagining that she was a man. That scared the hell out of me!

What was I to do? Had I made a terrible mistake in getting married? Could I somehow stifle the urges and go on?

We went on until, finally, the dam burst and, making up some excuse, I went to a gay bar. Of course I had, over the months, found out exactly where they were! The evening was successful, and I found myself repeating my "outing" every month or so.

By now, my frustrated physical desires were being replaced, not just by guilt, but guilt with a vengeance! Bad enough that I was ruining my own life, but what was I doing to Irene? I guess my acting abilities were in full force, because through it all, Irene seemed oblivious to my struggles, which only added to my angst.

I eventually had to admit to myself that I was unable to give up gay life, and that Irene deserved better than what I could ever give her. The burden quickly became more than I could bear and, when one day I found myself contemplating suicide, I decided it was time to try professional help again. Still, I felt I couldn't let Irene know the truth.

I managed to find an hour during each work-week when I could discretely visit the office of a Beverly Hills psychiatrist for a fifty-minute session. When I first entered his office, I passed a prominent male movie star leaving after a session just before mine. He's dead now, and never came out of the closet, so I won't mention his name, but he was well-known among the gay set as trying to go straight…as was I. Seeing him there each week just before my own session provided a glimmer of hope.

Everyone has heard these days about organizations that claim to turn gay men straight. Reputable psychiatrists will tell you that it doesn't work. Oh sure, any behavior can be repressed—for a time—but at an awful emotional price, and eventually the person's true nature will re-surface, the unwanted behavior often stronger than before.

Although my efforts with the psychiatrist didn't work, they did give me the strength to come clean with Irene and make the break, so that we each could try to find happiness elsewhere. Of course, that's much easier decided and said than done.

I desperately needed emotional support, and called upon my cousin, Feigie (short for *feigela*, meaning in Yiddish "little bird"), who was a large, motherly type to whom I had earlier confided my secret. Oddly enough, *feigela* is also Yiddish slang for a homosexual!

I asked for her help and she arrived just after I had made my full confession to Irene. I was feeling distraught and helpless in the face of Irene's tears, and Feigie was a great help to both of us. We all talked it out and agreed on a quick break as the best course: Irene went home to her parents, and I moved in with two gay friends who lived in Hollywood.

One, Mike Granger, an actor who had progressed to doing small roles in major movies, was already a close friend. Though we reacted to each other as "sisters," I always felt more like we were brothers—the way real brothers should be. He could be judgmental, but he was wise and compassionate, and I trusted him.

Irene and I filed for divorce. I could not object to her disclosing to her family the reason for our divorce. Her father, in particular, took it hard. In a letter from a lawyer, he demanded that I return the cash he had bestowed upon us as a wedding gift. I was too guilt-ridden to even think of refusing, but had no money at that point to comply, so I agreed to repay him in monthly installments. By the time I paid the last installment, I was preparing to marry again (more on that later!) and took satisfaction in mentioning that fact in the note that accompanied my final payment. As the spurned chorus girl says in the movies, " A girl has a right to some revenge, hasn't she?"

Before that time arrived, however, Irene requested that I come to Philadelphia for a Jewish divorce, in order to satisfy the Orthodox Jew she was about to marry. I was happy for her, though somewhat alarmed that her betrothed expressly did *not* want to meet me, but I went back.

Irene and I met for lunch before proceeding to the rabbi for the divorce ceremony, and she touched my heart when she looked at me across the table and said, in a sad, gentle tone, "You know, Sam, the years I spent with you were the happiest of my life. Are you sure we did the right thing in splitting up?" I had to look away to hide the tears that welled in my eyes.

When I looked back, I said, "Yes, Irene, I'm sure we did the right thing. You deserve to be loved completely and unconditionally, and try as I might, I could never give that to you." She nodded slowly, and we proceeded to the rabbi's chambers. I flew back to L.A. that evening.

It deeply bothered me that Irene's husband-to-be refused to meet me. I worried that it indicated an immature jealousy and/or resentment that could, in turn, mean a harsh possessiveness. From a rumor I heard later, it seems I was right. I told myself it was none of my business. I was no longer part of her life. Still, it remains one of my greatest regrets that I eventually lost contact with Irene. I hope, with all my heart, that she found the love and happiness she so much deserved.

One chapter of my life closed and another began.

ON THE TOWN

I was suddenly single and free to immerse myself in Hollywood's gay life, and I plunged in.

Discretion and repression were still the order of the times. L.A.'s police chief was upfront about considering overt gay activity in public to be immoral and illegal, and the notorious vice squad was actively raiding gay bars, looking for any slight infraction to close the place or haul off its patrons for "questioning." There were even plain-clothes detectives haunting gay bars, waiting for an unsuspecting patron to make a sexual proposition. The fear of being arrested—and thus publicly exposed—was constantly present in every gay's mind while at the bars. The fact that exactly the same sexual propositions were happening every night at straight singles bars was, at the same time, mostly ignored by the police and by the general public.

Nevertheless, the gay scene thrived. There were rumors of payoffs to local police, mob connections and influence at City Hall, but these were unverifiable. Whatever the reasons, there were gay bars throughout all of Los Angeles. Some were subdued and swanky—piano bars with romantic fireplaces were my favorite. Some had entertainment and floor shows, some "go-go" boys in briefs dancing on tables. Some had drag acts. Some were beer joints with pool tables, while others featured dancing to a juke box. One was even rumored to have a back room where sexual encounters took place, though I never knew anyone who confirmed that personally.

It all had one overriding purpose: to provide places where gay men could meet each other and make liaisons. At least that was my perspective. Another perhaps more important purpose was to provide an atmosphere where gays could enjoy an open camaraderie that wasn't possible in the straight world, where one had to be careful about what was said and how one acted.

Which brings up the subject of "swishy" behavior: At that time, the general public's perception of a gay man was a limp-wristed, prancing, mincing, effeminate-acting man. And they existed, but much of the time, it was an act that disappeared as soon as an audience was not looking. It took me a while to realize that this was more an act of rebellion than any kind of intrinsic behavior. Sure, it was fun to exaggerate feminine mannerisms, but most gay men didn't want to be a woman and most gay men were not really attracted to swishy types.

The "swish" was turned on and off at will. It was turned on, when the general public was looking, as a thumb-the-nose expression of defiance. It was also turned on, in private, with close friends, as a pressure-releasing mechanism. I tried it a few times, in private, but I was too self-conscious to carry it off well. Or maybe too inhibited? I understood why some gays enjoyed it, but I didn't need it. To each his own.

There were also more disreputable meeting places. It was well known that certain men's restrooms (for some reason unfathomable to me, gays often called them "tea rooms") were frequented by furtive types, who wanted quick, and occasionally dangerous, sex on the spot. The lure of sex in a place smelling of urine turned me off, but it seemed to be a favored activity for some married men who were hiding their homosexuality. The same was also true for some public bathhouses. Having sex there was quick and anonymous, but could be very dangerous because of the ever-possible presence of the vice squad.

This aspect of the vice squad's activities never completely disappeared, even after the harassment of gay bars mostly ceased. Witness today's headlines of prominent "heterosexual" men exposed when caught in the act in public restrooms or parks. The emergence of AIDS in the early 1980s, of course, brought a new deterrent to sex with strangers, a deterrent even more powerful than the threat from undercover detectives.

But this was pre-HIV, and I took to the gay bar world with passion. The thrill of conquest and of being desired was insatiable, and I hit the bars at least once a week. Now, however, in contrast to my earlier teen-age one-night affairs, I wanted more than sex. I wanted romance —hopefully even love. I wanted to find "Mr. Right."

My college had imbued me with the lofty aim of maintaining a conservative-medical-doctor image and demeanor, and that's exactly what I did in my role as a Doctor of Optometry. I had chosen the small but growing community of Pacific Palisades, and opened an upstairs office in a building just off the main street. Conventional advertising was not considered professional back then, so

I promoted myself by joining various local organizations, like the Lions' Club, where I roared with the rest.

Now and then, while tending my practice, some sweet older lady would invite me to dinner at her home and invariably (surprise!) also present would be a marriageable daughter or niece of roughly my age. I always accepted these invitations because it was an avenue of promoting my practice, but I had become more careful again to avoid any followup with these young ladies.

My double life went on, split between the professional me and the private me. I had become quite adept at it, and if it caused inner tension, I had learned to ignore it.

Back then, the big threat in the minds of idealistic youth was the atom bomb and global annihilation. One manifestation of that concern was the growth of an organization called the United World Federalists, which had the commendable aim of establishing one worldwide government based on love and brotherhood. There was a Pacific Palisades chapter, which I joined, not necessarily to promote my practice but because I believed in its lofty aims. I still do, though I have lost track of the organization and its activities. I recall attending one meeting at the home of David Niven, and another at the home of Joseph Cotten, both famous movie stars at the time.

At one World Federalist meeting, I met a very pretty divorcee who invited me to dinner one night at her home in the Palisades—with no mother or aunt to hover around us. After a lovely dinner, we moved to the couch to chat, and I felt obliged to make the expected overtures. So, we kissed…and I liked it! I never actually asked her out on a date, but we continued seeing each other occasionally at Federalist meetings. I respected her too much to play games, so I told her of my proclivity. To my surprise, she accepted it good-naturedly and we remained friends.

She later invited me to a cocktail party she was giving at her home, and I accepted. Among those present that night was Ronald Reagan, in his pre-politician days. He was recently divorced from Jane Wyman and now single. "Affable" was certainly the word to describe "Ronnie," as he was introduced to me. He hit it off with everybody. You couldn't help but like him. In those days he was a Democrat (did you know that?) and when I mentioned that I was planning to attend an upcoming meeting of the Americans For Democratic Action, he said he also was going to attend, and why didn't we meet beforehand and go there together? We did, in fact, but, sorry to disappoint, that was the full extent of our relationship. Years later, a lesbian friend of mine told me that a lesbian friend of hers swore that Reagan, in younger years, had a long love affair with her father, but I learned to take stories like that with a huge grain of salt. Some gays took great delight in including celebrities as "one of us," as if that somehow validated who we were.

Establishing a practice from scratch proved to be a longer process than I expected. My money was running out; I had already borrowed money from my brother, Meyer, and was loath to borrow more. I decided to cut my losses by closing the practice and getting a job working for another optometrist.

Within a few weeks, I was working in a commercial establishment in downtown Los Angeles. It was there that I first encountered Dick Mast, an optometrist from San Bernardino, who was seeking a partner to branch out and help operate multiple offices. My boss told Dick about me, and Dick and I met. Later, I met his wife and three children, whom I found pleasant and likeable.

Dick, however, had an irascible personality that took some getting used to. Short and squat in build, with a bulldog demeanor, he tended to criticize everything and everybody.

We proved to be about as opposite as possible. He had money; I had none. He lacked social skills; I was gregarious. He was ambitious; I was laid back. He was aggressive; I tended to be passive. I had every trait he lacked and he had every trait I lacked. It proved an ideal business match.

We quickly perfected a "Good Cop—Bad Cop" routine, which we used effectively later when we oversaw hundreds of employee-associates. Once, someone we fired remarked to a colleague, "Don't worry when Mast comes down on you, but if Gordon does, watch out—you're through!"

You can guess from that comment who did the actual firing. When I asked Dick why he couldn't do it, he simply said, "Oh, you're much better at those things than I am." I knew then that the tiger standing before me was really a pussycat at heart.

Our business partnership lasted more than fifty years. Oh, there were times I wanted to wring his neck, and I'm sure the reverse was also true, but as time went on, we became more like each other. Of course, I was careful to hide my "secret" from him, which proved easy to do because we never socialized outside of business functions. I guess we realized the dissimilarity of our natures and so, at least in the beginning years, kept our relationship "strictly business."

Meanwhile, nights and weekends, I was still looking for Mr. Right—with a distinct lack of success. My circle of gay friends wasn't wide enough to get me invited to many parties, so my avenue of making contacts remained mainly the gay bars. It took me several years to realize that singles bars didn't attract a lot of people looking for long-term, meaningful relationships. I was constantly disappointed to find that no one wanted to see me after a first encounter. At first, I thought it was me. Eventually it dawned on me that promiscuity was the name of the game at the bars...gay or straight.

I also realized, belatedly, that people who "put out" on the first date were not likely to be taken seriously. But, oh, how I yearned for romance, affection and—yes, real love—from a man. I know now I was too impatient...I wanted the miracle of love to happen right away. I know now that miracles like love happen, but infrequently. Which is why they are called miracles (Duh)! Still, I persevered.

For our first business venture, my new partner, Dr. Mast, chose Oxnard, which was about an hour's drive north of L.A. via the coast highway. I rented a little two-room shack north of upper Malibu, and made that my domicile while setting up and operating the Oxnard office. Dick had found a ground-floor location on one of the town's main streets, and it did well from the start, with a receptionist and myself staffing the office.

Once a week, I worked late at the office. On one of those nights, after closing, I decided to check out the small town square—a tiny park just one block from my office. Sure enough, there were gays "cruising" the park at night even in what was then a very small town. I connected with a sweet, shy young man and we had a tryst in my office. We encountered each other twice after that, but it didn't lead anywhere.

I also continued going to Hollywood and doing the bars on weekend evenings, getting nowhere in my romantic quest. What I *was* getting was disillusioned and dissatisfied. *If this is gay life*, I thought, *then I don't want it. Maybe I should devote my energies to business— making money—and forget about love. Maybe love was just a pipe dream, a scam invented by poets and authors to sell books.*

At that point, in a gay bar no less, Barbara whirled into my life.

My Two Wives and Three Husbands

S. Stanley Gordon

BARBARA

Barbara Posner flounced into my favorite upscale
gay lounge on the arm of Leon, a gay acquaintance of
mine. Leon was a "man about town," rich, suave, and
confident that he could bed any gay man he met—and he
usually did—but despite his attractiveness, his attitude
turned me off, so I remained one of the few who did not
succumb.

I do owe him a debt of gratitude, however, for
introducing me to Barbara, who was, and remains, one of
the most fascinating characters I have ever met. Barbara
had flair and poise that gave her an exotic sophistication.
She was striking and dramatic. Heads always turned
when she entered a room. Tall and slender, with jet-black
hair, she wore clothes like a professional model. So what
was she doing on Leon's arm in a gay bar?

Her life story is worth a book by itself, but here are the highlights as I came to know them.

Barbara's mother, Esther—a corruption of her real name, Anastasia—was a Yugoslavian refugee who, as a young girl, was put on a train during a World War I bombing raid, and ended up in Odessa. There, a Russian woman befriended her and assumed the role of mother to Esther and, later, of "Granny" to Barbara.

Esther and her "mother" subsequently emigrated to Shanghai and settled in the city's "international settlement." En route, however, they took a brief sojourn in Manila; brief but long enough for Esther to meet and marry an American merchant mariner, Ralph Posner, who accompanied them to Shanghai. Esther and Ralph sired a daughter, Barbara, and a son, Charlie. Esther contrived to get to the U.S. for each birth, to insure that they would be U.S. citizens, but immediately after always returned to Shanghai.

Being in the merchant marine meant Ralph got to see his Shanghai family only sporadically, for short visits. Eventually, even these visits ceased, as did all communication, and Esther was on her own. Attractive and feisty, Esther found work as a hostess in a Shanghai dance hall. I've always wondered about that "hostess" title and what other possibilities it might imply.

As Barbara told it, she was a willful, difficult adolescent. At seventeen, mainly to escape from her home life, Barbara married another Yugoslavian living in the settlement and proceeded to have a son, Barry. At which point, the Japanese invaded China.

Barbara's mother had dual citizenship (U.S. and Yugoslavian) but managed somehow to effectively hide the U.S. part from the Japanese, so she and Barbara's husband were not interned by the Japanese. Barbara and her brother, however, were ordered into a concentration camp, the U.S. and Japan being now officially at war. Barbara was suddenly faced with a difficult decision: she could take her son into the camp with her or leave him behind with her husband. She did what any loving mother would do, and left Barry in the care of his father.

Barbara never liked to talk about her time in the concentration camp, except to say that the conditions were terrible and the guards brutal. I assume that's when she developed a deep fear of men.

Several times before the war ended, Japan and the U.S. exchanged some token prisoners. Barbara's brother, Charlie, was among the first batch, and Barbara soon followed. Being dispatched directly from the concentration camp, she lost contact with her husband and son. According to Barbara, relations between her and her husband had, from the first, been rocky, and she later learned that after her departure from China he had obtained a Chinese divorce.

Barbara's mother was now living in America (Granny had died in China), and eventually mother and daughter hooked up and moved to Los Angeles, where they shared an apartment. Which brings me to that night in the gay bar.

A few words in private with Leon established that Barbara was straight and liked men, but had a fear of becoming sexually involved with them. She felt most comfortable in the company of gay men who posed no sexual threat.

That, of course, was fine with me, and I began taking her out occasionally. We enjoyed each other's company. I had just about given up hope of ever finding Mr. Right. Now, I found myself wondering if Barbara and I might be able to make a life together in a sexless marriage, with me being free to continue having gay affairs on the side —a selfish and arrogant request on my part. To my delight, Barbara agreed.

Wow! The best of both worlds, I thought.

Esther approved of the marriage wholeheartedly, though I think she never knew about the gay element involved. And so the decision was made.

I was still working in Oxnard and living in the shack in upper Malibu, so I would have to find a more suitable residence for the two of us.

By this time, I knew some movie people. One was a friend of the director, Lewis Milestone, who owned a small house on the beach not far from my shack and wanted to rent it out for at least a year. Serendipity!

The house was tiny or cozy, depending on how you looked at it, but big enough for two, and was, indeed, smack on the beach. Though rather isolated, being far north of the populated section of Malibu, the location was ideal for my Oxnard commutes, and the rent was within my means, so both deals were done: I signed the lease and Barbara and I eloped to Las Vegas.

Rather than remain alone at the beach house while I was working, Barbara elected to replace my receptionist at the office. We added a small dog to our little nest and life seemed complete. Except that life, at least for me, has a funny habit of turning expectations upside down.

We had entered our marriage with the understanding that we would make no sexual demands upon each other. Perhaps because of this, we were completely relaxed and comfortable with each other, so, of course, we began having occasional sex. Although, for me, it wasn't as wonderful as sex with a man, still it was pleasurable and I thought Barbara enjoyed it, too.

I particularly recall, early one balmy evening, acting out a stereotypic movie scene of the period and having sex out on our isolated beach. I am convinced that was the night when Barbara became pregnant.

There was no telephone service available to our house, so we let it be known to our friends that Sundays would be our "open house," drop-in day. On most Sundays, our little house was full of people, straight and gay. Dick Mast and his wife came by once or twice and, I discovered later, he was not as oblivious to my proclivity as I thought.

Our isolated stretch of beach encompassed one other small house close to us, which was owned by the movie actor, Lloyd Bridges, and his wife, Dottie, who occupied the place most weekends. Lloyd, whose nickname was "Bud," besides being an excellent actor, was gregarious and outgoing. Dottie was a warm and pleasant motherly type, and attractive to boot. We enjoyed having them as neighbors. They had two adorable sons: Beau (about eight years old) and Jeff (still in a crib), who later both followed in their father's footsteps. Their house, too, was lively on weekends, so often our groups would co-mingle.

Among the celebrities we met at the Bridges' were Betty Garret and Larry Parks, two sweet, lovely people, married to each other and deeply in love. I've encountered Betty now and then through the years, and she remembers those days as fondly as I do. Vivacious and pretty, Betty was an expert comedienne who had starred on Broadway and was featured in several movie musicals. Shortly before we met, however, her film career had been stymied because of her husband's travail.

Larry Parks had gained fame in movies, but had just gone through a terrible ordeal with the House Un-American Activities Committee. America was still in the throes of its Communist witch-hunting period, ferreting out supposed subversive influences who, according to the right-wing politicians of the day, were subtly undermining democracy. Hollywood was the ideal place to focus on, for its headline potential, and Larry was one of the actors accused of being, if not a Communist, at least a Communist sympathizer. The Unamerican Activities Committee told Parks he would be forgiven if he would give the names of industry people who he knew to be members of the Communist party.

One night, Larry and I had a private conversation about it. He had, after much agonizing, named names to the committee. The names he gave were already on the committee's list, but that didn't matter to Hollywood, which largely ostracized him. Some former friends stopped speaking to him and he could no longer find work in films. Betty was just on the verge of stardom, but she vowed only to work with Larry, so both of their careers were crippled. She staunchly kept her vow until he died, many years later.

Betty had a lively mother, who also visited occasionally. One Saturday night, when Betty, her mom and Larry were spending the weekend with the Bridges, everyone retired early except for Betty's mom, Barbara and myself. The three of us moved over to our house and began a game of cards. Shortly after midnight, still playing, we heard a knock on our door.

Who could that be at this hour in this isolated spot?

Was something wrong next door?

I hastened to the door, opened it and found myself staring at Gene Kelly. He looked surprised to see me, and asked if the Milestones were there. At which point, Betty's mother recognized his voice and yelled, "Come on in, Gene!"

It turned out that Gene thought the Milestones still were living there, and had come to invite them to go "grunion hunting" with him. Grunion are tiny fish that deposit their eggs ashore at that time of the year, riding an incoming wave, to be swept back to sea with the next. The sport was to go with buckets and flashlights, after midnight, and dash about, scooping them up before the next wave.

Accompanying Gene was a gamin of a girl— obviously a ballet dancer—who was in constant motion. She had a French accent but spoke little. Instead, she danced, pirouetted, leaped on the balustrade, and whirled about. She was delightful, and it was only later that I realized she was Leslie Caron, whom Gene had discovered in Paris and brought to Hollywood to appear with him in his upcoming movie, "An American in Paris."

Gathering up pails and flashlights, we all scampered

down to the water's edge to grab the grunion. They are supposed to be a delicacy, but the next day Barbara and I fried some for breakfast and decided their gastronomic reputation was vastly over-rated.

Sometime later at the office, I received a phone call from Washington DC. My brother, Meyer, lived there, so I hastened to the phone, expecting to hear his voice. Instead, it was Meyer's business partner who told me, tearfully, that my brother had been killed in a freak accident. He had been standing on the unfinished roof of the house he was building for himself and his family, when an overhead crane snapped and fell directly on him. I must have gone into shock, because all I could say was, "I can't think! I'll call you back." Barbara's mother happened to be visiting us at the time, and was in the back room where I had taken the call. I fell weeping into her arms.

Meyer was the only family member to whom I had confided my secret, so I felt a double loss. At the time, he had responded automatically with the then-culturally-correct suggestion that I seek psychiatric help, which he kindly offered to finance. After I explained the futility of that, he did some research of his own and became fully supportive, as did his wife, Marion.

Judaism requires burial within a few days, so the next morning found me on a plane to Washington. I had met Marion when she and Meyer were in Los Angeles some months before, and liked her. It was distressing to see her bedridden, pleading for someone to check the body to make certain it really was Meyer who had been cut down.

That crane had done a destructive job on Meyer's body, so the casket was closed. But, of course, the coroner had confirmed the identity, and soon we were able to convince Marion that her husband was, indeed, dead.

The situation was complicated by her being pregnant. Jews are not allowed to name a newborn after any living member of the immediate family (supposedly it "steals" that person's soul).

Marion's child was born a few weeks later and she named him Michael, in memory of his father, Meyer, who was sometimes called Mike.

Barbara, who was also pregnant, and I subsequently decided to also name our child, if a boy, Michael, in memory of the brother I had adored. It was a sad time, but life goes on and wounds heal, more or less.

Back to California and Barbara and our life together.

Barbara proved to be as good as her word. I had occasional trysts with men (never at our house), only to discover that Barbara had her own demons. For years, she had been subject to bouts of depression. Though short-lived and infrequent, they were increasingly disturbing to me, as well as to her.

It was during one of those down "moods" that she confessed that our sexual moments were not enjoyable, and that sex all her life had been a disappointment for her. How sad. She insisted she had no lesbian feelings. I felt helpless. On the other hand, we both looked to the birth and raising of our son as a mutually-shared emotional substitute.

Luckily, the business world intervened. It had always been Dick Mast's plan (and mine) to open more offices and it was time to implement that plan. Dick had found a good location in San Jose, so Barbara and I prepared to relocate. Barbara was now in the latter stages of her pregnancy. I hired a doctor and receptionist for the Oxnard office, found an apartment in San Jose and we made the move.

Both the new office and Barbara prospered, Barbara

64

giving birth to a healthy baby boy on November 6, 1951. We had finally become a real family.

My life was now full and I was busy, so I should have been content, but there remained an empty spot inside me which I tried to ignore. So, when I was approached to join a local amateur theatre group, I acquiesced and thoroughly enjoyed it. I used to joke about always wanting to be a "song and dance man" and was happy to pour some of my pent-up energies into acting on stage. Hadn't I been acting offstage most of my life anyway?

I even won a local award for the best performance of the year (a big-fish-in-a-little-pond scenario). The play was "The Time of Your Life," and, in the process of preparing, I had the chutzpa to write to the play's author, William Saroyan, regarding a question I had about the leading character's motivation. To my surprise, Saroyan answered me, albeit in a hastily scribbled note on a postcard. Still, I felt I was officially in show business!

A chilling aside: One day, two men, who looked like detectives right out of central casting, walked into my office and requested a word in private. After being seated in my examination room for privacy, they proceeded to tell me they were with the city attorney's office (or perhaps the local district attorney, I've forgotten which) and wanted to use our apartment to install a listening device on a common wall between our apartment and the adjacent one.

They explained that the two male teachers living there were suspected of being homosexuals (horrors!), and the detectives needed to tape their conversations. Moment of panic! Should I acquiesce to their outrageous demands in order to appear "straight," as many gay people at the time would? Or, if I say "No!" would my declining point a finger of suspicion at me? My hesitation was only for a moment, however. I knew I could never live with myself if I caved in.

My acting experience allowed me to react with just the right amount of righteous, all-American indignation. "Isn't your plan illegal? It sounds too much like the Gestapo, and I can't be a party to that." They did an about face, apologized for having taken my time, and beat a hasty retreat. When I got home later that day and related the story to Barbara, we agreed to alert the boys next door (whom we had gotten to know, casually, as neighbors), and we did. Shortly after that, we moved into a house we had just bought and never heard anymore about the two teachers, I'm sorry to say. Was it any wonder that gays in those days were careful to remain in the closet? Even the suspicion of being gay could cost love, job, even life.

My parents came out west to visit us for a week when Michael was about three. What a cute age that is, curious about everything and intensely aware of everything and everyone about them. My mom could be harshly critical and, with Barbara's high-strung temperament, I feared the worst. To my surprise all went well, perhaps because we were all so focused on little Michael.

Despite juggling my family, office and now thespian activities, I still managed to drive to San Francisco now and then for an evening's foray to the gay bars, and even to the married men's furtive favorite, the gay bathhouse.

By the time Michael was four, Barbara's depressions had become more frequent and more intense. It was evident that something had to be done, and we began seeing a psychiatrist, first jointly, then separately.

It took about a year for us to realize that a husband with another, separate, life was more of a traumatic burden than my wife could endure. Of course, we should have known better in the first place—maybe we even did, but later simply wanted so much more. We were increasingly fond of each other, but we decided, for both our sakes, to separate. Barbara and Michael moved to Mexico City, where (she reasoned) they could live better on the alimony and child support we agreed upon.

Parting from Barbara was a mixed muddle for me. My deep regret was intermingled with relief. Parting from Michael was gut-wrenching and caused pangs of guilt, but, I rationalized, he had had a doting father during his formative years, and we would always remain in contact.

When Dick Mast learned of the separation, as was inevitable, he asked me outright, while we were alone one day, if it might be because I was homosexual. At that time in my life, I was deep in the closet and fearful of losing the approval of anyone, let alone my business partner, so I replied, "Of course not...whatever would make you think such a thing?" He replied that, during those Sundays at my beach house, he had noticed the presence of obvious homosexuals.

I hastened to assure him that I had many such friends among the "actor" groups I knew, but that my problem with Barbara was due solely to her moods of depression. I should have realized that, if he was asking the question, he was already favorably disposed to hear the correct answer. But I was too fearful, and to Dick's credit, he didn't press the issue. In fact, he never raised the subject again, even though I'm sure he knew that I had not been truthful.

Once again I was "single" in the gay world, and where better to live that way than in the gay Mecca of San Francisco? I sold the house in San Jose and moved into an apartment in the city, from which I commuted daily to my office in San Jose.

Not wanting to stint on supporting Barbara and Michael, and at the same time finding myself severely strapped financially, I shared the apartment with a gay "sister," Ernie, whom I had known for years in Los Angeles and who was now living in San Francisco. He also was on a tight budget, and we literally penny-pinched—one movie a week, "nursed" beer at bars, chili and beans for lunch and dinner. While it sounds tough, looking back, it was actually a good life lesson: I learned how to get by on little.

Ernie had been a nightclub performer in his younger days, and he fed his greasepaint urges working evenings in San Francisco at a well-known club called "The Hungry I." He worked the backstage lighting board and announced each act. Occasionally, when Ernie was ill or too tired, I would substitute for him. Among the many performers and groups I recall introducing (via a backstage microphone) were The Limelighters, Odetta, Miriam Makeba, Mort Sahl and Maya Angelou (reciting poetry no less!).

I also remember a talented performer, who billed himself as "Professor Irwin Corey," who wowed the audiences each night with a brilliant routine, but then came backstage muttering about the patrons being "lousy bastards."

He reminded me of Charlie Chaplin. By all rights, he should have become a major star, but it never happened. I suspect his inner demons got in the way. What I learned from him was that talent alone was not enough. How tough this mistress called show business!

IT'S LOVE! IT'S LOVE!

It seemed to me, at this point, that my quest for Mr. Right was a fool's dream—elevated to the hopelessly absurd by the impossibility of realizing my goal. And yet...

One nondescript night, I was sitting on a barstool at one of my favorite haunts, a gay bar in San Francisco, when, gazing into the mirror behind the bar, I was suddenly struck by a pair of dark eyes. A face, strong and handsome, topped by thick, jet-black hair, animated by an alluring half-smile, made my heart flutter. *What an attractive man*, I immediately thought. Then, *was that a random glance or was he really "cruising" me?*

I looked away for a moment and then back. Sure enough, his eyes remained fixed on me, and now his half-smile was full and inviting. Smiling back, I turned on my stool to face him four stools away. Brushing aside my usual passivity, I picked up my half-finished drink and moved to the empty seat beside him.

Full of outward bravado and aplomb, I thrust out my right hand and said, "Hi! My name is Stanley," though inwardly I was trembling. His was the most appealing face I had ever encountered. He appeared about my age and height, and was wearing a dark grey suit with a white shirt, open at the collar. If he had had a tie and a briefcase, I would have pegged him as a young executive.

Thrusting forward a steady, confident hand, he replied, "Hello, there! I'm Hank," and we began to talk.

He was, indeed, a junior executive, on temporary assignment from his job in New York, due to return there a few weeks hence. Oh well, I thought, another pickup at a bar, another one-night stand, like countless others before it.

He stayed the night at my apartment and surprised me the next day by agreeing to spend all of it (Sunday) with me. In fact, we were together every night during the following week, and subsequent weeks as well. It didn't take me long to realize that I had fallen in love: hopelessly, completely, unreservedly, for the very first time in my life. I was astonished to discover that the poets hadn't lied. The sky really *was* bluer, the grass greener, the birds' songs more beautiful! Everything around me sparkled and glowed. My heart sang. Here I was, in my thirties, and in the throes of first true love! My heart had told me my prince would come, and here he was, at last.

Our time together was spent simply. Hank was on an expense account and insisted on paying for our dinners. Otherwise, we went to the movies, or stayed in and watched television, went for walks, or just sat and talked. And, of course, made love. Oh, how we made love!

Why this man, I asked myself, *and not any of the countless men before him*? I had no sensible answer. I only knew that I was hopelessly smitten. And better, Hank felt the same way…or so he said at the time. We proceeded to lay plans: He was living with a man in New York whom he didn't love. His corporate employer had an office in San Francisco, and Hank would arrange a permanent transfer as soon as he returned to New York. Life was exciting and brimming with promise, something I had never entirely felt with anyone before.

Inevitably, the time came for Hank's return East. At the airport, our farewell was heart-wrenchingly emotional…we both cried, though our tears were tempered by the knowledge that our parting was to be only temporary.

Hank warned me that it would take time for him to accomplish the necessary changes, and I promised to be patient. He asked that I not contact him until he had cleared things with his (ex?) lover, and said he would let me know as soon as they separated. That alone should have been a warning bell, but I wasn't about to allow anything to dampen my gloriously overflowing elation.

Three weeks passed and I heard nothing. *Well*, I told myself, *breaking up is hard to do, and I resolved to be the patient, understanding lover as promised.*

Business matters took me to Los Angeles for a few days, during which time I visited my cousin and alter-mom, Feigie. As I excitedly told Feigie the good news, she listened quietly. When I had at last finished, smiling, awaiting her reciprocal reaction, she simply asked how long it had been since I had last heard from him.

"More than a month," I stated.

Feigie looked at me sadly and gently replied, "You'll never hear from him again."

"Oh, no!" I wailed like a wounded animal. "That just

can't be! I couldn't bear it!" I continued, rejecting the thought vehemently. Life couldn't be that cruel! Hank's tears at our parting were real…I hadn't imagined them! No, no. It was just taking longer than expected.

After another month went by with no word, I began to feel a sinking sensation. I had promised that I would not contact him, but now I had to know the truth. I knew where he worked and called him. His secretary said he was out of the office, so I left a message, giving my home and office numbers. After two more days of silence, I telephoned again. "Yes," his secretary said, she had given him the message. We checked the numbers I had given her. They were correct. She would give him the message again.

Silence.

As the days passed, the awful truth dawned on me. I went cold and numb inside. How could I live without him? Numbness soon gave way to despair, and despair to desolation. Never had I known such devastation. During the day, I was able to function, keeping busy, but oh, the nights! I cried myself to sleep every night. Looking back from my present vantage point, I realize this was "first love," like teenagers painfully experience and never forget. Was this delayed, adolescent heartbreak? I don't think I will ever really know. All I know for certain is that I had loved him, unconditionally, with all of my body, heart and soul.

At this point, business again intervened.

A new type of discount department store had appeared in cities throughout the country, catering to government employees and requiring an annual "membership" fee. Of course, the definition of "government employee" was almost infinitely broad, including teachers, postal workers—if a fourth cousin twice removed had such a job, the whole family seemed eligible.

Some large corporations, like Woolworth and National Bellas Hess, were wanting to get into the act, too. Dick Mast had been talking with the owners of just such a store that was about to open in Sacramento, with a view to leasing space for an optometry office. Dick and I discussed the idea with a number of our optometric peers, who mostly dismissed the notion as being professionally demeaning. Our friends thought that, if it truly was such a good idea, someone else would have done it by now. That's what did it for us: After all, if no one else had done it, how could anyone know it was a bad idea? Dick and I decided to plunge ahead.

We reasoned that, since I was single, I would be the one to move to Sacramento, set up the office and operate it. I leaped at the opportunity to drown my sorrows in work. We sold the San Jose office and I made the move to Sacramento.

For this new endeavor, I kept long store hours: 10 a.m. to 9 p.m., six days a week, plus 10 a.m. to 5 p.m. on Sundays. *Wow!* I thought. *I'm outdoing my father!*

I was the on-duty doctor all those hours, and, frankly, it felt good to keep busy. Oh, I still cried myself to sleep every night—it would take almost a year for that to stop —but I had the new office to focus on during the day.

Our success was immediate and exceeded all expectations. It didn't take long for the news to reach owners of other similar department stores, and we began to receive requests to open optometry offices under similar conditions in several different states.

Dick was always the go-getter, the spark plug, and I was always the willing, subservient partner. Dick had a family and family responsibilities in Pacific Palisades; I was single and free. Our first office in this endeavor, under my direction, was a smashing success. It therefore made sense that I would be the one to open the future

77

offices, which suited me just fine. Love had dealt me a dirty blow, so now, by God, I was going to devote myself entirely to making money. To hell with love!

What happened to Hank? A friend of mine met Hank at a party in New York a few years later, and told Hank of the anguish I had gone through. Hank apparently showed little or no reaction. Apparently his returning "home" had given our intense sojourn together a different perspective. *For him, in the end, it had been just a "summer romance."*

In New York quite a few years later, I was walking along Madison Avenue and literally bumped into him! He greeted me amicably and suggested that we stop and have coffee at a nearby shop. I thought, *Why not? After all these years, I can be civilized about it.*

I learned from him that he was still with the same job and partner. Then he took my breath away by propositioning me: We could get a hotel room, then and there! I was aghast. Was this shallow cad the same man for whom I had, and, yes, still had deep feelings? I sprang to my feet, and with all the dignity I could muster, said, "That will never happen. Good bye," and I walked out, leaving him sitting there with a stunned expression…and the check.

Working seven days a week at the Sacramento office distracted me from the pain in my heart, but it eventually began taking its toll on me, so I hired a doctor to replace me on Saturdays. This left me free to drive into San Francisco for an occasional short "weekend." I could leave Sacramento Saturday morning, drive for two hours, spend the rest of that day and evening in the city, and drive back to Sacramento in time to be at the office when it opened at noon on Sunday.

Meanwhile, Barbara and Michael had moved back to San Francisco. Barbara found a job as office manager at the office of two plastic surgeons, and Michael was enrolled in public school.

I made it a point, with Barbara's okay, to spend Saturday afternoons and early evenings with Michael. Usually, we had dinner and saw a movie together, or sometimes had an outing to Golden Gate Park or Fisherman's Wharf. It gave Barbara a chance to have some much-needed time on her own. We agreed that I would have Michael home by 9 or 10 p.m. on Saturday night—leaving just enough time for me to hit a few gay bars.

One late night in particular still haunts me: I had met

a young man with whom I had made a date to meet at 10:30 p.m. this Saturday night. I eagerly anticipated the evening, but as luck would have it, Barbara happened to be late getting home that night, so Michael and I sat in my car and waited. She arrived at 10:30, full of apologies. No problem, I assured her, my date would surely wait a half hour for me. Still, I was anxious to be on my way and wasted no time in making my goodbyes and driving off.

As I was driving away, I happened to look in my rear-view mirror. Michael was standing at the curb, hands in pockets, looking dejectedly at my retreating car with an expression of such longing that I felt my heart cry out —Barbara must have been standing beside him, but the picture etched in my memory is that of a forlorn-looking little boy.

At the next corner, I turned out of view, pulled over to the curb and tried to stem the tears that filled my eyes. He seemed to be saying, "Why are you leaving me? Come back. I need you!" Every fiber of my being told me to go back, to wrap him in my arms and reassure him.

But I didn't.

Instead, I rationalized that if I went back, it would

simply mean a second, perhaps even more painful parting. He had to adjust to the reality of things as they were, as they had to be. So I drove off, stifling my urge to go back. But every time that image returns—and it often still does—I wish I had gone back.

I wish I had. I wish I had…

My Two Wives and Three Husbands

THE WHIRLWIND

When the Sacramento office was firmly established, I hired another doctor to replace me and moved on to create several offices in the greater Los Angeles area. My friend, Mike Granger, with whom I had lived after separating from my first wife, Irene, was living alone in Hollywood, and his apartment became my base of operations while I opened an office in a store in West Los Angeles, and then several more in other suburbs of L.A.

Mike was making his living as an actor, playing small roles in movies. He was compassionate and charismatic, and our apartment became the hub of an interesting assortment of aspiring "movie people," including actors, writers, directors and would-be producers.

My straight friend from Philadelphia, Martin Kanter,

was also living in West Los Angeles with his new wife, Charlotte. I introduced them to Mike and some of our crowd, and we all became instant friends. In fact, the Kanter residence became a second social hub for a smaller group, including me, who met there for dinner parties and parlor games.

A new craze was sweeping Hollywood at the time— self-analysis—and our little group took it up with an eager zest. Most of us were "hams" after all, and self-analysis provided dramatic, sometimes histrionic confessions that made for stellar party entertainment. We took turns, and what began as fun and games often morphed into serious self-introspection. Many a tear was shed. I realize now that the process provided me with a much-needed catharsis to work out the end of my relationship with Hank, my marriage to Barbara and the wrenching separation from my son. So it did at least one of us some good. I think.

Mike and I were more than roommates but less than lovers, although many people considered us both. We cared a great deal about each other and we were as close as brothers.

Coincidentally, about the same time that I fell in love

with Hank, love marched into Mike's life—for the very first and, sadly, only time in his life. The man he loved ended up rejecting him, and Mike ended up going through a similar period of despondency as I had. Boy, did I know that feeling! His misery was interrupted by his being cast in a small role in a film called "The Conqueror," starring John Wayne and Susan Hayward. It was being shot on location for six weeks in a remote part of Utah, near St. George.

I was happy for him because I knew that, like my work, it would distract him from his sorrow. How fortuitous, I thought. Little did either of us know what was actually in store for him there.

By the time I had fully moved in with Mike, the shoot in Utah was over and forgotten, but suddenly he developed morning sickness, like a pregnant woman. When the nausea persisted and progressed to several times a day, Mike began seeing doctors. Every test proved negative. They could find nothing physical that could cause his increasingly severe symptoms, and eventually decided it had to be "psychosomatic." Being the romantic I am, I assumed it was the result of his grieving over unrequited love, but his sick days persisted and his work began suffering as a result, though somehow he managed to carry on.

A few years later, Dick Powell, who had directed "The Conqueror," died of cancer. Subsequently, both Susan Hayward and John Wayne died of cancer. Then another cast member died of cancer. No one thought to make the connection, but years later, when Mike moved to New York, barely able to make ends meet doing part-time voice-overs, he was contacted by a filmmaker who was preparing a documentary on what happened to the cast and crew of "The Conqueror." By that time, nearly every member of the cast and crew who had been on location in Utah had either died of cancer or was seriously ill from a mysterious ailment. It turns out that the government had conducted tests on the effects of atomic radiation on cattle in Nevada a year prior to the shoot, and the radioactive cloud had drifted into Utah. Some people knew about it, but no one realized how dangerous it could be.

Mike died soon after that, from "undiagnosed causes," while in his early fifties. That documentary never appeared, to my knowledge.

While Mike was ailing, I had my hands full, opening offices, not just in California, but now throughout the country. Between 1958 and 1963, Dick and I established fifty offices in seventeen states, and I personally opened most. Looking back, it seems impossible, but I did it. Living in motel rooms and furnished apartments, I criss-crossed the country setting up, staffing and doing the necessary training for each. Not knowing it was impossible, I just went ahead and did it!

My days were long and filled with myriad tasks. Some of the preliminary construction work would have been done in advance, but I now had to meet with the local workmen to supervise the completion of each office build-out.

In those days, very few optometry offices had their own facilities for fabricating eyeglasses, so most doctors used one of two national wholesale laboratories. The one we used was American Optical Company. As such, my first stop in any new city was to meet with the local manager of that firm. He knew the best opticians in town and how much they were earning. He also knew which doctors were unhappy in their jobs, or had practices that were floundering. That made personnel recruitment easier.

In addition, the discount department stores in which we were placing our offices had files on potential receptionists, so that was no problem.

I reserved lunches to interview and entice opticians. Dinners were for doctors and their wives—I quickly learned that the "little woman" was instrumental in a doctor's decision! In between, I set up the optical equipment, purchased office furniture and ordered supplies. In addition, I had to be sure to attend daily meetings with store management. My days were full to the brim, and most evenings I was content to crawl into bed after dinner.

On weekend nights, however, I was free to carouse! Even as a stranger in a new town, it was not difficult to find a gay bar, despite the fact that such bars were still a very hush-hush topic for the public. I discovered that, for some reason which eludes me, almost every city had a gay bar within a one-block radius of the Greyhound bus station, and the bartender at that one bar afforded information on all the gay spots in town.

Occasionally, when that system didn't work, I had merely to engage a taxicab and ask the driver to take me to the nearest gay bar. Taxi drivers always knew about such things!

Love? Never heard of it! I was immune to love,

having become the proverbial traveling salesman sporting strictly one night stands. I had graduated from teen-age to adult slut. Perhaps "slut" is too harsh a word. A slut will sleep with anyone. I had my standards and returned to my apartment alone more often than not.

I was also becoming more aware of the lurking dangers of casual encounters. Besides vice squad entrapment, there were crazies out there! Somehow, I was always able, after some conversation, to avoid these bad experiences waiting to happen. Was a sixth sense at work here?

There was one time when I made an exception to my one-night stand rule, and, interestingly, I came to regret it. It was my first weekend in Denver, and I connected with John, a sweet, gentle, attractive guy who was in his late twenties—younger than I at the time. We were instantly attracted to each other and, after a few hours socializing at the bar, we went to my motel room. He stayed the night and I felt that we had developed a real rapport, so when he invited me to lunch at his home to meet the two lady friends with whom he shared his house, I accepted.

The two ladies turned out to be lesbian lovers. They were from Germany, like John, and very personable. We had a pleasant lunch, after which the ladies excused themselves. As they were leaving, however, one of them made a laughing remark to John, which I didn't entirely catch. But I did hear a reference to the "SS," and I froze.

John was old enough to have served in the German army during World War II, so when we were alone, I asked him, "What was that reference to the SS? Were you a storm trooper during the war?"

"Not quite," he answered. "I was sixteen when I was conscripted into the army as a foot soldier. But I was given the opportunity to better myself by becoming an SS trainee."

"John," I said, looking him straight in the eye, "I am Jewish."

"So?" he replied innocently.

"So, as part of your training, weren't you taught to despise Jews?"

I shivered inside as he placed his hand over mine. "Not everyone believed the Nazi propaganda. There were many of us who didn't go along with it, but they were in power, so there was little we could do about it."

He seemed entirely sincere. I knew there had to have been "good Germans." But still, if the war *hadn't* ended the way it did, John, as an SS member, might have ended up committing heinous acts.

I tried during the remainder of the visit to be accepting, but I simply couldn't. I made my farewell and never saw him again. Even now my flesh crawls when I think that I had sex with an SS man—though only a trainee, or so I was told. It's hard for me—especially as a gay Jew—to forgive and forget what happened in Germany: the wholesale public slaughter of Jews, homosexuals, Gypsies, and anyone else the Nazis deemed inferior. I knew it could happen again, anywhere, under the right circumstances, but the fact remains that it definitely happened there and John had been a part of it. Up to now, I purposely hadn't set foot in Germany, and when I finally did, in the late 1990's, I looked searchingly into the faces of the milling throngs on the streets of Berlin. I don't know exactly what I expected to see, but most of these people were either born after the war, or had been but toddlers at that time. I shouldn't condemn an entire society for the sins of the fathers. At least, I kept telling myself that.

Anyway, my work-and-play routine continued in city after city. Occasionally, I would meet Dick Mast at some resort to attend a convention of NACO (National

Association of Consumer Organizations), the umbrella trade organization for the member discount department stores with which we were involved. These were mostly social outings, where I mingled with older, conservative business people. I had to blend in, pretending to care about the latest baseball scores and stock market reports. I must have been successful, because I remember at one point one of the gruffer men clapping me on the shoulder and saying, "You're smart and I can see you like girls. You're alright in my book!" Shudder!

In which city it was eludes me, but I recall while setting up an office I had occasion to consult a medical doctor for some minor ailment. During the course of the consultation, the doctor inquired about my activities, so I told him about my cross-country optical endeavors. He gave the customary doctor's "Mmmmm," but then, after giving me a prescription, startled me by saying, "Does your company need money? I'd like to invest."

"Isn't that a bit rash?" I said in return. "You don't know anything, really, about my company."

To which he promptly replied, "I don't invest in things or companies. I invest in people. You are a winner. I'd like to invest in you."

I was deeply flattered, naturally, but told him that we weren't in need of funds. He gave me his card anyway, saying, "Well, if you ever are, contact me."

Back at my latest apartment, I casually tossed his card away, totally unaware that years later, as a Broadway producer, I could gladly have made good use of his offer.

My Two Wives and Three Husbands

EMMETT

By 1961, Dick Mast and I had hired regional managers. We decided that Dick would supervise the western half of the country from his home in Southern California, while I would handle the eastern half from a new executive office in New York City, which I was to set up.

My old friend from high school, Sid, was now living in Manhattan and offered to share his apartment. I accepted, for the time being, planning on making more permanent arrangements later, but before that could happen, lo and behold—you guessed it—love found me again!

There have been times when, at first sight, the hairs on my body stood on end for no apparent reason...and experience has taught me to rightly beware of those people. Conversely, now and then, I met someone to whom I immediately felt attracted. Sometimes, it turned out to be simple lust. Other times it turned out to be a feeling of warmth and comfort. Once in a fortuitous while it might be both. All-too-rarely, these two would be accompanied by an indefinable glow inside that said, "This person is *very* special." That was how I felt when I met Emmett Rogers.

I could sense Emmett felt something similar, too, and we immediately struck up an easy conversation. Emmett was no Adonis and a few years my senior, but he had the kind of gentle, trustworthy face and demeanor that I found greatly appealing. His manner was gentlemanly and charming. His hair was thinning, and he was dressed casually and conservatively. I couldn't guess his occupation, though it turned out that he was a Broadway producer—a revelation that normally would have struck me dumb with awe. Instead, we were totally at ease with each other. He invited me to drop in at his office "some time," and gave me his office number.

Two days later, I found myself in the vicinity and stopped by unannounced—cell phones not being in use at the time. It was late afternoon, and he was alone in his small office in the Paramount Building.

Our visit was polite, but as we talked, I became aware of a feeling of expectancy, a slight breathlessness. Then suddenly, he kissed me! Not with passion but not with awkwardness. It was with a sweetness that made my head reel. *It's only a kiss*, I told myself. *So why are your knees buckling and why are there butterflies in your stomach?* my sixth sense interjected. Trying to be oh-so-nonchalant, I smiled and—not knowing what to do—said I had to leave.

For the next two hours, I walked the streets of Manhattan in a daze, mostly talking to myself. *What is this feeling?* It wasn't the wild elation I felt with Hank, but I was definitely knocked for a loop. Could *this* be love? *Was I ready to risk the even greater vulnerability that I sensed would come with it? And, besides, what if he really felt nothing for me*—but I knew that was a lie. Soon after I returned to Sid's apartment, Emmett called to apologize. "I'm sorry if I startled you. I hope I haven't scared you off. I really want to get to know you better. Please forgive me."

Before I could think, I replied, "There's nothing to forgive. It was quite alright." Excited but cautious, I refrained from adding, "I liked it."

"Would you come to my apartment tomorrow afternoon, for tea?" Today was Friday; the weekend lay just ahead. And, once again, *what's with the tea?*

"Sure," I said with only a moment's hesitation. "What time?"

He quickly gave me a time and address.

The conversation ended politely, with more casualness than I felt. I was certain I could sense a similar feeling of hopeful anticipation on the other end. As I hung up, I saw Sid, hands on hips, eyebrows raised, waiting for me to expound, so I regaled him with the day's event, feeling free to express the excitement I had been holding in since Emmett's kiss. Even though he had never met Emmett, Sid was as thrilled as I at the romantic aspect of it all.

The next day, I arrived at Emmett's apartment where we talked, drank a little—cocktails, not tea—and talked a lot more. We both knew that we had to see each other again, so we made the first of what proved to be many dates. I believe we both felt from the start that we were in love, though neither of us would admit it until six weeks later, when he asked me to move in with him at his apartment in the Dakota. Which I did.

Though I had, of course, heard of the Manhattan apartment building, until I lived there I did not appreciate its fame. In later years, it would become famous as the place in front of which John Lennon was shot, but it had always been well known to New York celebrities, especially creative artists. Built in 1884 at the corner of 72nd Street and Central Park West, then surrounded by fields, it stood solitary and remote from the nearest residence—which may have given rise to its name. It was an instant success, and the rest of New York soon built up around it. Built like a fortress, it had thick walls and large apartments with high ceilings.

Originally, the first nine floors were luxurious apartments, the tenth floor being given over to a large playroom and gymnasium. Sometime later, the tenth floor was divided into "smaller" apartments of four or five rooms each (!), and it was one of these that Emmett was renting. Emmett and the noted British Shakespearean actor, Maurice Evans, had lived there as lovers, and when they broke up, Evans moved elsewhere. Prior to their occupancy, it had been the New York *pied-a-terre* for Boris Karloff, the famous actor who played the monster in the movie "Frankenstein."

Emmett had retained a friendship with the Karloffs,

so I had occasion to spend some time with Boris and his wife, Evie. Contrary to his screen image, Boris Karloff was a gentle, retiring, sweet man; his wife was a charming and warm English lady.

The building had four elevators, one in each corner wing. We shared our elevator with several famous stage and screen actors, Lauren Bacall, Jason Robards, Judy Holiday and Zachary Scott, among others. Once, I rode down with a handsome British actor who was starring on Broadway. His name, Keith Michell, was not well known in America, but I had seen his show and had been impressed with his talent. Little did I know how our paths would cross again in later years.

Emmett and I were deliciously happy. I spent part of my working day in my new office on 57th Street and the rest of my day in Emmett's office in the Paramount Building, where I eagerly soaked up everything I could about show business. Emmett had co-produced (with Maurice Evans) the Broadway hits "Teahouse of the August Moon" and "No Time For Sergeants," and had then produced, on his own, a hit comedy, "Tall Story," which became a motion picture starring Tony Perkins.

Talent agents would occasionally "drop by"

throughout the day to introduce a client to be "remembered" for future casting. I recall one such visit by an enthusiastic agent whose client, though attractive enough, was so shy, and looked so frightened that I felt sorry seeing him so uncomfortable. His name was Robert Redford.

Then there was the young writer who had provided the lyrics to two hit Broadway musicals, but whose main aspiration was to write both the lyrics *and* music for a show. He came to our apartment for drinks one Sunday afternoon and told us about an outrageous idea he was toying with, a comedy, taking place in ancient Rome. Of course, the man was Stephen Sondheim, and the show he wrote both music and lyrics for was "A Funny Thing Happened On the Way to the Forum." Emmett was interested, but apparently the well-known Broadway impresario, Harold Prince, already had an inside track on producing that musical.

I was still in the throes of opening optical offices, so I was gone for short periods, though always back in New York for the weekends. We were fortunate to be so happy together, I thought.

But then, after some months, Emmett created a quiet and private moment to tell me that, after much soul-searching, he realized that he did not love me! Just like that. While I sat, speechless, he continued: "I know now that my feelings were influenced by the fact that you had money and knew people who could be potential investors. I feel awful that I deceived you and myself. We have to part." I was back in all-too-familiar shock, so I'm not at all sure I'm quoting him accurately, but that was the gist of it. His demeanor was calm, even stoic.

I was stunned. At first, I refused to believe my ears. "But Emmett, you've met many other people with more money than I have, and you haven't thought you loved any of them. And there's nothing wrong with my affluence playing a part in your attraction to me. I think you are feeling guilty needlessly."

It was his turn to go silent, so I went on, "After all, part of my attraction to you may have been your show business background. Still I've met plenty of other show people without falling in love with any of them."

He listened, but in the end, he was adamant. And what was more, he wanted me to move out that very day!

Like an automaton, I packed my bags and moved back with Sid. How could I explain Emmett's behavior? *There must be someone else,* I thought. That would make sense, at least. Otherwise, it would have to be something about us. What had happened to my sixth sense? I was bewildered.

Ten nights later, Sid answered his telephone, hung up, turned to me and said, "Emmett is around the corner and is coming up to see you." My first reaction was to refuse to see him, but then I thought, *that's childish*—and there was the unfinished sense of our relationship hovering over me. I needed to find out what he wanted. So, he was admitted and, to my (and Sid's) astonishment, he immediately went down on his knees and begged my forgiveness. On his knees! My absence made him realize how wrong he had been, he said. He loved me desperately, he said, ending with, "Please, please, come back!" There were genuine tears in his eyes.

Sid rolled his eyes, but I was hooked. How could I refuse such a romantic plea, especially when I so wanted —needed—to believe my own intuition? So back I went. Was I being stupid? Was I blinding myself to a deep flaw in Emmett or myself? I brushed aside all such thoughts. I loved him, and that was all that really mattered.

After that, all went well between us, just as though that nutty interlude had never occurred. Soon, I was able to put it entirely out of mind.

The offices I rented on 57th Street were a converted two-story apartment. My private office was extremely large and imposing, so I suggested to Emmett that he give up his Paramount Building quarters and share my office, which he did. Now I could spend full time taking care of my business and my avocation together, and I began spending an increasing amount of my latter time reading scripts. One day, I heard Emmett laughing out loud. Looking at him, seated at his desk across the room, I saw him with a script in his hand. He gave it to me saying, "This was written by a zany stagehand who worked on one of my shows, and I think it has possibilities. What do you think?" It had the *non sequitur* title, "Thursday Is A Good Night."

Although the script initially struck me as slight, it was funny in an offbeat kind of way. Emmett suggested that I get my feet wet by co-producing it with him, in a tryout tour in what is known in theatrical circles as summer stock.

Summer stock meant a tour of eight to ten weeks, during the summer months, performing the play in theatres situated in key East Coast resort locations. This meant mainly Catskill and Pocono mountain resorts, and in an established circuit of small theatres in northeastern states. The cost was mostly subsidized by the theatres, so it was relatively low. There was little or no money to be made as producers, but it would get the play in front of live audiences so we could decide if we wanted to mount a full production for Broadway.

The legendary director, George Abbott, had a daughter, Judy, who had worked beside her father and who was anxious to forge her own career as a director. She liked the script, so we engaged her. She invited us to have dinner one night at her apartment, where her father would also be present. Emmett and I assumed he wanted to add his stamp of approval.

The night before the dinner, I prepared by reading George Abbott's recently-published book, in which he bemoaned, "Why does everyone call me 'Mr. Abbott?' Why doesn't anyone ever call me 'George'?" So at one point during dinner, after Mr. Abbott had held forth for some time and finally said something that required an answer—I've forgotten what the question was— I began with, "Well, George..." I've also forgotten the rest of my reply, but what I do remember, vividly, was the look on his face as I said "George." His head snapped up and he fixed me with the most withering look I have ever seen. I wanted to disappear under the table. Too late, I thought to myself, *That's why no one ever calls him "George!"* He must have forgiven me, though, because he didn't scotch our deal with his daughter.

That funny actor, Tom Ewell, noted for his role in the movie "Seven Year Itch" with Marilyn Monroe, was available and liked the script. We also engaged the services of Sheree North, who was being groomed by Twentieth Century Fox as a possible replacement for Monroe. A comic actor, Joe Bova, was cast in a supporting role. Sheree North, usually cast in blonde bombshell roles, proved anything but dumb. Sweet and down-to-earth, she proved very bright and a joy to work with.

Tom Ewell, on the other hand, seemed edgy and needed careful handling. Luckily, Judy Abbott was up to the task. Rehearsals went smoothly, as did the entire tour.

It soon became evident to Emmett and me that, although the show had its moments, it was not of Broadway caliber, so we let it die a natural death. The best thing that came out of the run was Judy Abbott and Joe Bova falling in love and later getting married.

Six months later, we found another script we both

liked, titled "Madame Mousse," jointly written by the French heartthrob, Jean-Pierre Aumont, and Eric Segal, author of the bestseller, "Love Story." Jean-Pierre wanted to play the lead and was willing to do a tryout run in summer stock. The play was a lighthearted whimsy about a daffy French mother and her family. We thought that Word Baker, who had directed the long-running "The Fantastics," would be just right to direct our soufflé, so he was engaged.

We needed one more big name to draw the summer audiences, and I had the offbeat notion of asking Molly Picon, the darling of the Yiddish stage, who had recently starred in Jerry Herman's "Milk and Honey" on Broadway. Molly was intrigued with the idea of playing against type and accepted.

Molly did a very credible job transforming herself from a Yiddish to a French Mama. The entire cast, in fact, was excellent, though the play, in the end, refused to come together. In show parlance, it just didn't "work."

Molly Picon's contract called for her to do the play on Broadway, but she was smart enough to see what a turkey we had and asked to be released from her contract at the end of the summer stock run. Of course, we agreed. My second production tryout suffered a quiet, natural death.

A small role in the production was played by the wonderful, and very old, English actress, Estelle Winwood, who was temporarily living with the "*grande dame* of the theatre," Tallulah Bankhead. Tallulah was noted for her nicotine-and-whiskey-tinged gravelly voice and her outrageous outbursts. An oft-quoted remark of hers was, "Bisexual? Of *course* I'm bisexual, dahling. *Buy* me something and I'll be *sexual*!" Several times, I met Tallulah when I picked up Estelle Winwood to escort her to rehearsals.

Some time later, I was at a party when Tallulah sauntered up to say hello to someone I was talking to. As my friend started to introduce me to Tallulah, I said, "Oh, we've met before when I came by your apartment to pick up Estelle Winwood. Do you remember me?" She of the withering remark barked, "Of *course* I remember you, dahling, and aren't you *ashamed* of yourself?" To which I could only laugh and reply, "As a matter of fact, I am...it was *not* a good play." An epitaph that's funny to a play that wasn't.

I learned from that play that, in order for a production to be successful, all elements must jell—

script, cast, direction, sets, costumes. If *any* element goes wrong, it won't work. No wonder there are more flops than hits. A big-enough star can draw enough ticket buyers to keep a mediocre production running, but only for a while, as I was to experience later.

So, Emmett and I were back to reading scripts. I occasionally left town to open another optical office. Living at the Dakota had become comfortable for me and was definitely glamorous.

One party at that fabled building will stick forever in my memory: We were invited to cocktails by actors Ruth Ford and Zachary Scott, a married couple whom Emmett knew and who maintained a large apartment at the Dakota. Their expansive living room was studded with celebrities from stage and screen. When, after a few hours, Emmett and I decided to leave, our hostess escorted us to her front door and, just as she was reaching for the doorknob, the doorbell rang. When she opened the door, we found ourselves looking at an elderly gentleman and no less than Greta Garbo! During introductions, she exuded charm and graciousness, but what I remember most was that she literally glowed. That built-in, elusive thing we call "star quality" simply emanated in every direction with incandescent brilliance.

Of course, Emmett and I immediately changed our minds about leaving and trailed behind back into the living room. The conversation level in the room had been building, but the moment Garbo entered, the entire room hushed. Even the biggest of the big names in the room were awed in the presence of the Great Garbo.

We soon optioned a comedy by screenwriter Robert Presnell, Jr. We ended up dropping it, but not before we met Presnell's wife, beautiful screen actress Marsha Hunt, who was to become another of my lifelong friends.

Marsha had been a successful model before being signed for the movies. She had starred in some good "B" movies, played supporting roles in some "A" films, and was being groomed by MGM to become a major star. One of those "A" films was "Pride and Prejudice," starring Laurence Olivier. Marsha played, of all things, an ugly duckling. With wig, makeup, false teeth and good acting, she was able to transform herself, but I thought it was ridiculous casting. Marsha, however, said she loved playing it.

Unfortunately, the Presnells had flown with the first planeload of Hollywood celebrities to Washington DC to protest the House Un-American Activities Committee, during the national "red hunt" scare of the early fifties. They had never been, nor considered themselves, Communists, but felt it their duty to protest the distinctly un-American tactics of the committee. Bigger stars on that plane, like Humphrey Bogart and Lauren Bacall, made too much money for the studios to be blacklisted, but Marsha was put on the unofficial but potent blacklist, pretty well ending her promising career in films. She went on, however, to become a volunteer emissary for our country at the United Nations, where she served for many years on several committees to good effect.

To this day, Marsha and I remain good friends. Her beloved husband died, but Marsha has retained her razor-sharp memory and her gracious wit, as well as her stunning looks, even now well into her nineties. Quite a lady!

One day, Emmett gave me a book instead of a script to read. Written by William Peter Blatty (who wrote "The Exorcist"), the novel, entitled "John Goldfarb, Please Come Home," was a whimsical comedy about an Arab sultan and his harem. Emmett thought it could be fashioned into a comic musical for Broadway, and sent it to the great choreographer and director, Jerome Robbins of "On the Town" and "Fiddler On the Roof" fame, whom

Emmett knew.

Jerry, as his friends called him, reacted positively, so Emmett and I called the publisher to option the dramatic rights. To our surprise, we were informed that movie star Shirley MacLaine had already bought the rights with a view toward making it into a straight (non-musical) film.

Well, we thought, perhaps we could all get together and do the Broadway musical with MacLaine in the starring role, after which she could do the film version. Jerry liked the idea and called Shirley, who said she was interested. She would be in New York for a few days soon, and asked that we contact her at her New York hotel at that time. I suppose she wanted to see if we were compatible.

Emmett and I picked up Shirley at her hotel and we went to dinner together. We spent a pleasant evening, chatting amiably. We seemed to see eye-to-eye on the tone of the show, and I thought all was well. Alas, several weeks later, Jerry reported that Shirley had decided to forgo the stage production, opting instead to proceed with her straight film version. Much later, the movie, with Peter Ustinov playing the potent potentate, opened to tepid reviews and poor box office receipts. I must confess that its being less than a wild success gave me some satisfaction. I still think it could have succeeded as a musical, especially with the great Jerome Robbins at its helm.

My Two Wives and Three Husbands

BROADWAY

At last, Emmett came across a script that he considered to be ideal Broadway material. Entitled "Her Apron Strings," it was a comedic account of an Irish mother who dominated—and thereby complicated—the attempts of her three sons, all New York policemen, to find love and marriage. Emmett felt we should skip the summer stock circuit and go directly for a short pre-Broadway run in Boston, then open on the Great White Way.

Now, a producer's first task is to raise the money. Emmett had a list of interested investors from his previous Broadway hits, but this small, low-key comedy by an unknown author didn't get a great response: After two months of fundraising, we had only raised half of our required capital—including a substantial contribution from me. Emmett's funds were low, so he was unable to contribute much in terms of his own money.

One afternoon, after exhausting our list and leads, Emmett sat at his desk and wept with frustration. We seemed to be at a dead end. Putting our heads together, I recalled another producer who had mentioned a Chicago businessman who had made a large investment in a show a few years ago. I called our producer-friend for permission to contact his source, and was given his name and phone number.

The man's name was W. Clement Stone. We knew nothing else about him, except that he had made his fortune in insurance. Later, we learned that he was a big contributor to the Republican Party and was the patron saint of the Chicago Lyric Opera. He was a busy, much sought-after man, positioned unreachably behind banks of secretaries who screened all calls. To this day, I have no idea why, but when I dialed the number I had been given, he answered the phone personally. Providence?

After identifying myself and explaining how I obtained his name and number, I asked if he might be interested in another Broadway investment. He was terse and to the point: "How much money are you looking for?" I tried to sound nonchalant as I mentioned a figure that represented all of the remaining capital we needed. "Send me the script and budget," he said and gave me an address. No other questions or comments. It didn't sound hopeful, but I wasted no time in sending him the material.

Three days later—I remember it was late afternoon on a Friday—the phone rang in our office and I happened to answer it.

"Stanley Gordon?" the voice asked.

"Speaking," I replied.

"Clem Stone here." For a moment, I honestly could not remember who Clem Stone might be, but then it came to me. "I like the script. I'll be in New York next week. Meet me at ten o'clock on Tuesday morning at my hotel," and named an eastside hotel.

"We'll be there," I replied. "We're looking forward to meeting you in person, Mr. Stone."

"Call me Clem," he said, adding, "A deal's a deal," and hung up.

Recounting the conversation to Emmett, I couldn't help but wonder what exactly Clem meant by, "A deal's a deal." While we both had lots of guesses—ranging from frivolous to the sinister—the best course, we decided, was to simply wait until we met with him.

Tuesday morning, we discovered what he meant when he blithely handed us a check for the full amount we needed. Clem Stone was a brisk, vital, smallish person, with sparkling eyes and a pencil-thin mustache. He had written several self-help books about the power of positive thinking and handed a copy of one to us. We offered to give him billing as "Associate Producer," and he accepted. Whew!

We had completed the capitalization; the next step was to engage a director, and Emmett gave the script expectantly to Jack Landau. Jack liked the play, and came on board. I did not know Landau's work at the time, but Emmett thought highly of him and that was good enough for me. The three of us agreed that the title lacked punch, so we spent the next few days dreaming up—and discarding—dozens of possible titles. As I thought about the play and its meddling mother, who was always reading the riot act to her sons, the title came to me: "The Riot Act." That was it, we all agreed. Now for the casting.

Thelma Ritter was our unanimous first choice for the mother. She had always been cast in movies as a lovable but acid-tongued supporting player, and she was perfect for our annoying but well-meaning mother. Alas, at our meeting with her and her agent, she politely but firmly turned us down, saying she was afraid to take the leading role and all the responsibility it entailed for "carrying" the play. I realized later that Emmett and I dropped the ball badly...she had wanted us to talk her into it. Why else would she have agreed to meet with us? But, stupidly, we accepted her at her word. It was also a huge misstep on her part. Had she succeeded in this starring role on Broadway her career would have zoomed. Instead, it gradually declined. Such is fate.

Emmett personally knew the "First Lady" of the American stage, Helen Hayes, and, though she wasn't really right for the role, we sent her the script. She, ever gracious, told us that she admired the play but felt the role was not for her. Of course, she was right.

We needed a "name," or at least a semi-name, who would attract theatre goers, and our next choice was Dorothy Stickney, who had played the mother in the long-running stage play "Life With Father." She, too, was not ideal casting for the role, but she was a talented actress who we felt could quite possibly carry it off. Another plus was her husband, Howard Lindsey, who had co-authored "Life With Father," and might conceivably be valuable to our neophyte author during the inevitable

119

out-of-town re-writing process. Happily, Dorothy agreed to play the role!

Another important role was the mother's close friend, a tough but funny, wisecracking commentator of ongoing events. I immediately thought of Ruth Donnelly, who had played the smart-ass telephone operator or secretary in almost every Warner Brothers movie during the thirties, forties and fifties. She was now retired, but we managed to contact her and she agreed to meet with us. She was exactly what we wanted, and we signed her.

Casting for the three sons and their girlfriends was a process largely presided over by our director, who had no compunction against his producers sitting in and conferring on the final selections. Auditions went on for several weeks before we finalized our choices and cast six young newcomers to Broadway. One actress particularly impressed us during her audition readings. She went on, in subsequent years, to become a major star of the New York stage. That was Linda Lavin, who later gained national fame as the star of the television series, "Alice."

We cast, as another of the "girlfriends," a buxom blonde named Sylvia Miles, who later made a name for herself by dumping a loaded plate of spaghetti on the head of a prominent theatre critic noted for his venomous reviews. Ah, show business!

The remaining roles filled quickly. Every actor who auditioned for Emmett was impressed with his thoughtfulness. Each and every one who was not cast received a handwritten note from him the following day, thanking the actor for auditioning and wishing him or her good luck next time. I don't know of any other producer or director who took the time and trouble to do that.

Rehearsals went well and, all too soon, we were ready for our opening night in Boston. The show went well and the audience was responsive. A few hours later, Emmett, our director Jack Landau, the author Will Greene, and I gathered up the early morning editions of the local newspapers and retired to our quarters in the Ritz Hotel to read the reviews.

Three of the four reviews were mildly positive, but the fourth, by the most influential critic, Elliott Norton, was scathing. "A sad little, bad little play opened last night at the Wilbur Theatre," he wrote. That's as far as I got before giving way to despair. Norton's "thumbs down" was usually the kiss of death, especially to a new play. There was nothing to do, however, but persevere and hope.

Clem Stone came to Boston and met with the entire cast after witnessing a performance. He was upbeat and encouraging, giving each cast member a copy of his latest self-help book. He didn't know that, just prior to the performance he witnessed, I had directed Sylvia Miles to tone down the one action in the play that might have conceivably been ribald enough to offend Clem's conservative sensibilities.

We showed him the reviews, pointing out that, if we closed the show now, some of the still-unspent monies could be returned to him. Clem, however, was undaunted, so after some re-writing, we prepared for our New York opening.

Although Elliott Norton was usually a reliable harbinger of what the New York critics would say, there had been a little comedy two years prior called "Visit To A Small Planet" that had been severely panned by Norton, and went on to win the plaudits of New York's critics and even won some awards. We clung to the hope that history might repeat itself, but fate intervened. We were in the last days of previews before the official opening when, suddenly, all of the New York newspapers went on strike.

We lacked the financial means to prolong the previews, having no idea of how long the strike might last, so we went ahead with our opening night as planned, counting on the television reviewers to save us from oblivion.

Both television and newspaper critics showed up, but our hope that the strike would end in a few days so that their reviews might still be published died a slow and very painful death.

The TV reviews were actually fairly positive, and one was especially good, so, in line with Clem's advice in his books, we continued to hold on to our hopes. Audiences were largely enthusiastic, and Ruth Donnelly gave an after-curtain speech each performance, asking the viewers to spread the word.

Even so, without the newspaper critics' still-unpublished endorsements, ticket sales slowly diminished and, after a few weeks, Emmett and I decided to close the show while there was still some money to be returned to Clem and the other investors.

Later, our press agent managed to get a copy of what the Times' critic wrote. He gave us a mild pan, but said that Ruth Donnelly should be cast in the next fifty comedies done on Broadway. Poor Ruth! If the review had appeared in print, she might have had a great second career. As it was, she retreated to Hollywood and, as far as I know, lived a quiet life until her death.

The failure of "The Riot Act" had a profound effect on Emmett.

I was busy running the optical enterprise with my New York staff, and occasionally flying to Los Angeles for meetings with Dick Mast. Emmett, however, seemed to shrink within himself. His usual courteous demeanor was maintained in daylight hours, but nighttime brought a surliness to the surface. He began drinking more than before—still, only at night—but his increasingly erratic behavior began to worry me.

Another worry arose from the optical chain Dick and I had created. The "membership" department stores that we were placing them in were slowly being eroded by other merchandising outlets, and I could see the writing on the wall. So I began urging Dick to talk with his Dallas friend, Dr. Stanley Pearle, about buying us out.

Pearle had "gone public" with a stock issue, on our recommendation, some years prior. His chain, known as "Pearle Optical," had, in turn, been acquired by a larger company, G. D. Searle. I convinced Dick that the time was ripe for us to enter into negotiations with the Pearle/Searle team.

So, post "Riot Act," I ended up flying back and forth to Texas for buy-out talks. Twice, during these meetings, I was called away to take a telephone call from Emmett, who drunkenly demanded that I return home. Each time, I managed to placate him, but it frightened me to imagine the new path our life was taking.

Soon, Dick and I came to an agreement with Pearle and the purchase was consummated. This meant eliminating our New York staff and closing down the office, so Emmett and I moved our stage production office to a two-room office suite on Seventh Avenue.

Now, I had money. Not a fortune, but more than I had ever known before.

I'm not sure if this contributed to Emmett's personal sense of failure, but his behavior worsened. By day, he was still pleasant, but by night he became someone else —verbally-abusive to anyone close at hand. Then, one night, he struck me with a resounding open-handed slap to my face.

It happened during a dinner party at the Los Angeles home of my "self-analysis" friends, Charlotte and Marty

125

Kanter. Aghast, I looked from person to person and uttered, "I don't know what to do!"

"Hit him back," volunteered one of the guests. Stupidly, I made a half-hearted attempt, while Emmett shielded his head with his hands.

We sat in frozen silence until Charlotte, ever the practical one, said, "Well, we can't pretend that didn't happen, because it did!"

"Why did you do that?" I asked, turning to Emmett. He muttered, almost unintelligibly, that he thought he had heard me use a curse word. Needless to say, we excused ourselves from the party and beat a hasty retreat.

Looking back, the alcohol was destroying him. It was certainly destroying our relationship. The most frighteningly curious thing, however, was that he never showed the slightest remorse, and refused to discuss the incident or alcohol. I knew enough about alcoholism to know that pleading with him to seek professional help would be to no avail, but I pleaded anyway, while he coolly dismissed my pleas, one after another. He seemed to divide into two different people, a veritable Jekyll by day and Hyde by night.

I have always abhorred violence, and I warned

Emmett that, if he ever raised a hand to me again, I would leave. So, of course, he did just that one night when we were alone in our apartment. Without saying a word, I went into the bedroom, locked the door and lay on the bed, thinking. I never heard him trying the door, but I heard him crawling on the floor by the door, and I visualized him peering through the crack under it. Eventually, all sound ceased. I had decided by then that I would leave first thing in the morning.

By this time, the Dakota had converted from rentals to cooperatives, and I had purchased our apartment in both our names. That wasn't going to stop me, however, from moving out. I couldn't move back with Sid, because he now had a lover living with him and I didn't want to intrude, so I called another good friend, Wynn, who was living alone in a two-bedroom apartment on the eastside. He assured me I was welcome.

I packed a suitcase while still in the locked bedroom, and then quietly walked through the hallway toward the front door. Emmett was asleep on the living room couch. I hastily scribbled a note, saying I couldn't go on this way, and included Wynn's phone number, with no other comment, and left.

That day, I refrained from going to our office,

instead, staying at Wynn's. I guess I was waiting for Emmett's phone call, which never came. Was I relieved or disappointed? I wasn't at all sure.

The following day, I showed up at the office. Emmett was there, in his room, reading a script. I poked my head in, said, "Hello," and went to my own desk in the adjoining room to await his next move. It never came. He acted cool and distant, as though we were business acquaintances who happened to be sharing office space.

Things remained that way for two weeks, until, one day, he failed to appear. I thought nothing about it, but a few days later, when he still hadn't shown up, I became concerned.

Calling a mutual friend, I was informed that Emmett had admitted himself to the psychiatric wing of New York Hospital. I asked if Emmett had requested that I be informed, and he said, "No…. I assumed you knew."

Hooray! I thought. He's finally seeking help! A good, positive sign that there was still hope!

Now, it was my turn to face things. I was still undecided as to how to proceed. Should I hasten to his side? Should I play it cool, and be his concerned friend? Should I wait to hear from him?

Two weeks went by with no word from him, so I finally called the hospital to ask if I could visit him. They gave me the visiting hours. When I finally saw him, Emmett was quiet and detached, with little to say. Well, I reasoned, he must be under sedation or other drug therapy.

I made my decision and behaved like a supportive, casual friend, engaging in nebulous small talk, trying to feel my way. I made the customary inquiries. He was under the care of a resident psychiatrist; I asked, and Emmett told me the doctor's name. I made a mental note, and asked if there was anything I could do for him. No, he said, there was nothing he needed.

Emmett had no family, so there was no one to notify. I gave him Wynn's phone number again, and asked that he call me if he needed or wanted anything.

Two more weeks went by and, having heard nothing, I made a second visit, which went exactly like the first.

Several weeks after that, I sought a private meeting with Emmett's doctor, which was arranged. It was a meeting I will never forget.

The doctor was younger than I expected, and surprisingly forthright and authoritative. Of course, he knew all about me and my relationship with Emmett, so there was no need for any pussyfooting around.

"Doctor," I said, "I want to do everything I can to help Emmett get well. It seems to me that I should move back into the apartment, tell Emmett that I am there, and wait for him to come home, regardless of how long it takes."

To my surprise, the doctor shook his head vehemently. "No, no, no. That's the worst thing you could do. Mr. Rogers has to learn to rely on himself, to stand on his own two feet, to cope independently."

"That sounds like a long process," I ventured hesitantly.

"Not necessarily," he replied with customary medical detachment. "But I will not release him until I am certain he is ready."

Every gut feeling inside told me this doctor was wrong, but how could I refute an expert? Surely he knew best.

"Okay," I replied. "Here are phone numbers where you can reach me. I would appreciate being notified when that happens."

"I will do that," he promised, "but until then, I think it best if you had no further contact with him."

"And after?"

"After, of course, you can make contact, but I strongly suggest you proceed slowly and begin by seeing if you two can re-establish a relationship. If you are able to do so, be aware that the new relationship may turn out to be quite different from what you had before."

I was uneasy with his words, but accepted his advice. I nodded and left.

Then I waited. And waited.

Two months went by with no word. Then one day, the same friend who had advised me of Emmett's admission to the hospital, called to say that Emmett had been released the previous week.

Why hadn't his doctor called me? I was angry and frustrated.

What to do next? How to proceed? Heeding the doctor's advice to proceed slowly, I decided I would wait another three days. If Emmett hadn't called me by then or shown up at the office, I would call him.

On the evening before the third day, I was sitting in a restaurant, waiting for a friend to show up for a dinner date we had made. He was late, and as I peeked at my watch, I felt someone tap me on my shoulder. Looking up and around, I was surprised to see Wynn standing there.

"Come outside," he whispered. "Someone there wants to see you." How odd, I thought, but went with him. Outside, Wynn admitted that he had lied about someone wanting to see me in order to get me to leave the restaurant quietly. "Why?" I uttered. "What's wrong?"

"Emmett…killed himself. Two detectives are waiting at the Dakota to interview you." I remember thinking, *how can Wynn be so calm in the face of this thunderbolt?* Then I began to tremble. I am vaguely aware of Wynn's pulling me into a waiting taxi for the drive to the Dakota, but my mind was reeling. I must have gone into a state of shock, because what happened next was like a movie witnessed on the silver screen from a distance.

As we entered the apartment, the first thing I saw was our part-time maid and cook, Gertrude, standing in the vestibule, crying. Wynn guided me into the den, where two men in suits were standing. I definitely was not prepared for this sight: papers strewn everywhere; Emmett's body slumped in an armchair; telltale pills and alcohol scattered on the floor beneath his lifeless hand. I had assumed that his body would have already been removed. The sight made me cry out, "Oh, my God!" and I averted my face from the horror.

The detectives waited a few moments for me to regain some composure, then said, "As Mr. Rogers has no family to claim the body, we thought you would want to make the funeral arrangements." *How do they know all about me?* I wondered, but there was no time to follow the thought.

Somehow, I managed to name a funeral parlor in New York, and one of the men said he would call them. Then he added, "Mr. Rogers left this note for you." He handed me a small sealed envelope, on the front of which Emmett had written "Stanley."

I quickly thrust the note into my pocket and mumbled something about needing to go to the bathroom.

After locking the bathroom door, I shakily opened the envelope and read the note. In Emmett's handwriting, it said, "Stanley: I can't go on without you. Please forgive me." I crumbled with grief, while at the same time somehow reaching inside of myself and rallying.

My first thought was what I should do with the note. A vision of tomorrow's *New York Times* floated before me: "Noted Broadway Producer Commits Suicide Over Failed Homosexual Love Affair!" I couldn't let that happen to Emmett's reputation.

As the detectives hadn't asked about its contents

133

when they handed me the note, my first instinct was to rip it into pieces and flush it down the toilet. But that might induce questions, especially if the police, coroner or court —oh, yes, there would surely be a public inquiry into his death— asked for it later. Instead of flushing it, I slipped it in my pocket and emerged, stunned, from the bathroom.

Wynn somehow managed to extricate both of us and get me back to his apartment, where several friends were waiting to console me. I showed them the note. It shocked me back into emotional oblivion. I vaguely recall asking if they thought I should destroy it. They all agreed that I should keep it. It was important "evidence" that the law would undoubtedly need, given how closely entwined Emmett's and my business, financial and domestic affairs were.

Sure enough, less than an hour later, Wynn's doorbell rang and he admitted the two detectives. "We forgot to get the note from you," one of them said. "We need to retain it."

I handed over the envelope, and we all watched while the first detective opened it and silently read the note. He refolded the note, carefully put it back into the envelope, and placed the envelope in his pocket. Then he looked directly at me.

I girded myself for a homophobic reaction, but he said gently, "I'm sorry for your loss." The two left without another word, leaving me numb and shaking, but relieved that I ultimately had done the right thing with the note.

My Two Wives and Three Husbands

LONDON

The next few days were a total blur, but I was peripherally aware that Wynn was providing a lot of help. I had to retrieve all of the papers Emmett had strewn across his desk before taking the pills and alcohol: his birth certificate, army discharge papers, insurance records and a short, handwritten will—leaving whatever he possessed to me. More guilt! I remember wondering for a moment what Emmett's psychiatrist must be thinking. I almost called him, but decided against it. The man would, I hope, be wrestling with his own guilt just now.

Emmett's funeral was a quiet affair, but well-attended by industry colleagues and friends. Everyone treated me as the "next of kin," and expressed their condolences. It surprised me that, throughout it all, I remained so stoic; no tears, just never-ending regret that our love had failed, and Emmett had lost his way.

A chapter in my life had ended. Again love had failed me.

I concentrated on not looking back, but nagging thoughts kept surfacing: Was I to blame? Should I have defied the doctor and followed my instincts? And why did I wait three days? If I had waited only one day, or even two days, things might have turned out differently. Over the next few weeks, I came to realize that dwelling on the "what if's" was simply a futile exercise in self-blame. I *had* to move on.

I decided to move back into the Dakota and try resuming my life.

What had been Emmett's room at our offices on Seventh Avenue was poignantly vacant, so I rented it to a woman, Selma Tamber, personal manager to several stage costume designers, as well as to choreographer Hanya Holm, best-known for her Broadway, and later movie, accomplishment, "My Fair Lady."

Selma Tamber's no-nonsense, brisk personality, along with her warm, down-to-earth wisdom, made her endearing yet formidable. Always impeccably dressed, her prematurely-gray hair perfectly coiffed, she was a middle-aged widow who lived in a small apartment in one of Manhattan's upscale hotels. We quickly became fast friends as well as office-mates.

Scripts were still being submitted, and eventually Selma and I found one we both liked, entitled "Possibilities." Two friends of Selma's joined us in mounting the production off-Broadway.

Though no star names were cast this time, I suggested to my co-producers that we ask the renowned set designer, Jo Melzeiner, who lived at the Dakota, to do our small production. "Are you crazy?" was their reaction. "He gets big bucks doing top Broadway plays. Why would he ever consider doing anything for the peanuts we could pay?" Undaunted, I went ahead and asked him. After reading the script, he accepted. Later, when a reporter asked Melzeiner why he had never before designed an off-Broadway production, he replied matter-of-factly, "Because no one ever asked me."

Even before opening night, however, we knew we had a turkey on our hands—the show didn't work. I was never able to pinpoint what went wrong; the elements simply refused to gel.

The *Times* critic gave it a one-sentence review that made me burst out laughing: "'Possibilities' is a no-no." I guess he, too, couldn't analyze why. We closed after one performance.

It was my intention to remain at the Dakota, but over the next few months, the constant reminders of that terrible night proved too much, so when a director I had met offered to purchase my apartment for double what I had paid for it, I accepted.

Not wanting to impose on Wynn again, I answered an ad in the *Times*, placed by someone looking for a man to share his penthouse apartment on West 55th Street. It turned out to be a spacious, two-bedroom layout with great views of the city on two sides. The occupant was Donald Pippin, a Broadway music director, who was currently conducting the orchestra for "Mame," starring Angela Lansbury, on Broadway.

Donald and I agreed on terms, including sharing of the facilities, and I moved in. We each kept our own schedules, and our lives were pretty much separate. I wasn't sure if he was gay or straight, but either way it didn't matter—we judiciously respected each other's privacy.

Back at the office, my attention returned to a project that Emmett and I had started just before his death.

Screenwriter and author Anita Loos (of "Gentlemen Prefer Blondes" fame) had written an adaptation of a French comedy about Henry the Eighth and his fourth wife, Anne of Cleves, which had had a successful run in Paris. She adapted it with her pal, Carol Channing, in mind, but Carol had by this time fully embarked upon what was to be her lifelong career with "Hello, Dolly."

The play's title was "The King's Mare." Emmett and I had interested the corpulent British actor, Robert Morley, in playing Henry, and Morley recently informed me that he wanted to open the play in his native London first, before New York. I agreed, though I knew little about the London stage world.

Providentially, I was visited at my office by singer/ actor Jerry Wayne, who wanted to become a producer. He had spent a year in London, having discussions with noted English stage producer, Donald Alberry, about the two of them co-producing a musical version of "A Tale of Two Cities." Jerry needed financial backing in order to proceed, and offered to bring me in as third co-producer on the show. I heard rumors that Jerry had been blacklisted during the infamous Un-American Activities Committee shenanigans, and had moved to London as a consequence. I also knew from Marsha Hunt's experience that many innocents had been smeared with the "red" blacklist brush, so I gave it no further thought.

What I desperately needed was to get away, so off I went with Wayne to London to meet with Alberry. For some reason, the British producer wanted to postpone the "Two Cities" musical, and instead waxed enthusiastic about "The King's Mare," which, of course, was fine with me. Donald Alberry would open all the necessary doors for me in London, and this was exactly the break I needed. No papers were signed; instead, we made a gentlemen's agreement to all three co-produce the play.

For the role of Anne of Cleves, Alberry suggested (and procured) Dora Bryan, a current favorite comedienne of the London stage.

I rented a large flat in London's theatre district that had space for an office staff, as well as living quarters for Jerry Wayne, his local girlfriend and myself. The flat had formerly belonged to Ivor Novello, who had been the reigning writer, performer and producer of London musicals. Located directly above and adjacent to the famous Strand Theatre, it seemed providential. Rumor even had it that Novello had a peephole in his flat through which he could see the stage of the theatre, but apparently it had been plastered over after he died.

To illustrate the vagaries of show business, our star, Robert Morley, suddenly decided against doing "The King's Mare," for reasons I never ascertained! Dora Bryan was still committed, though Alberry had not yet drawn up her contract. Now, who to play Henry?

Keith Michell immediately came to mind. Having seen him perform in New York, I knew he was a talented actor, but could he transform himself from a slim, handsome leading man into a corpulent Henry? I contacted him and we met for lunch after I sent him the script. There was no doubt in his mind that he could play the part, and that was good enough for me.

Alberry was pleased with the news and promised to draw up contracts for both Keith and Dora. But he dithered: every few days, I would call his office, only to be told the papers were still being prepared, not to worry.

Then, out of the blue, Dora Bryan was offered the role of "Dolly" in an imminent production for London, and she chose it instead of ours. So now we had our Henry, but no Anne. In the meantime, our English director withdrew in favor of another project.

I began to smell a rat, and the rat turned out to be Donald Alberry, who had decided to abandon us without informing us of that detail.

By that time, Jerry and I had hired our office staff, so we decided to carry on by ourselves. We engaged another director, Peter Coe, who had directed "Oliver Twist," and we started our search for a box office "name" to play opposite Keith Michell.

The heavens must have blessed us, for we received the wonderful news that, due to the efforts of our author, Anita Loos, and her actress-friend, Cathleen Nesbitt, London theatre's "favorite daughter," Glynis Johns, had agreed to come to London and star in our play. The Johns family had a long tradition on the London stage, and Glynis had not performed locally for many years, being busy acting in Hollywood films. I was delighted to have her services, despite warnings from several sources that Glynis could be "difficult and unreliable." I never paid much heed to such scuttlebutt, reasoning that every story had two sides, and was determined that, given our situation, Glynis deserved the benefit of the doubt.

Upon her return to London, along with her husband, Elliott Arnold, I saw immediately where those warnings had originated. Glynis wasn't "difficult," she was frightened and insecure. She needed careful, attentive "handling," which Elliott, an author with a solidness about him that calmed his nervous wife, provided. He was the "anchor" she needed.

Glynis was a marvelous actress, and I quickly came to adore her. At every performance, she would stand in the wings waiting for her cue, trembling with stage fright. But the moment she set foot on stage, she transformed into a "Rock of Gibraltar," acting with a strength and assurance that amazed me. Better yet, the audiences loved her.

Keith, good to his word, transformed himself into a wonderful Henry, so much so that people from the BBC, seeing his performance during our run, cast him in a later series about Henry and all of his wives, which successfully aired worldwide, including on PBS in the U.S.

Peter Coe finished assembling an excellent supporting cast, and rehearsals began. Our out-of-town tour had been charted, with theatres booked in Liverpool, Brighton and Golders Green, a small town just outside of London.

Long before rehearsals began, we submitted our script, as required, to the Lord Chamberlain at Buckingham Palace for official approval (a euphemism for royal "censorship"). Hearing nothing from his office, we assumed all was well. But—lo and behold—we received word from him, a week before starting our tour, that a pivotal scene in our play was forbidden. It was the "bedroom" scene, with Henry and Anne in and out of bed, and was absolutely essential. The Lord Chamberlain had decreed, however, that we could not portray royalty in bed together. Oh, wow! What to do?

The next day, Peter Coe, Anita Loos and I poured into a taxi and hastened over to Buckingham Palace. On the way, Anita said, " Every time I've had a run-in with censors, I've ended up with something naughtier than before. I have an idea."

Before she could tell us her idea, we had arrived at the palace and were ushered into the office of the Lord Chamberlain, who firmly reiterated his objection. For a long moment, there was silence all around, and I inwardly despaired. Then Anita spoke up. "Suppose," she said, "we play that part of the scene in the dark, so the audience will hear but not see what's transpiring." Oh, I thought, he'll never go for that, but to my surprise, he said cheerfully, "*That* would be fine."

And that's the way we did the scene. Anita was right.

In the dark, with the audiences' imagination in play, the scene was twice as funny…and suggestive! So much for censorship!

Prevailing producer-wisdom sternly warned, "always use other peoples' money to finance a show, never your own," but my biggest failing as a producer was my reluctance to ask people for money. I hated that aspect. So I defied prevailing wisdom, and financed "The King's Mare" entirely myself! After the show in Liverpool, I heaved a big sigh of relief: We were a smash, with glowing reviews and cheering audiences; this in spite of the fact that I worried about a weak second act.

When we hit Brighton, a more sophisticated town with a famously tough critic, her review savaged us. Still, we did brisk business and moved on to our last engagement before London, Golders Green.

Jerry and I commiserated over the Brighton critic's review, and soon the weak second act began occupying all our thoughts. Golders Green was only an hour's drive from London, and over the course of that run, we brought in two directors to see and critique the play, in the hope that one might come up with a brilliant idea to strengthen the second act. One thought the show was fine "as is," and advised us to leave it alone at this late date. The other agreed about the weakness of the second act, but could offer no immediate solution, so we moved on to London for the official West End opening.

The opening was set for a seven o'clock curtain. Peter Coe had arranged for the cast to do an afternoon "run through," just to keep them occupied and less inclined to be nervous. Anita Loos was already aware of an international array of her celebrity friends who had flown into London for the opening.

That afternoon, while I was soaking in the tub in my flat, Jerry knocked frantically on the door, shouting that Glynis was in hospital! At one point in the play, she was required to leap from the bed, over the footboard, and onto the floor. It had never been a problem before, but during the run-through that afternoon, she tripped on the footboard, broke a toe and injured her shoulder.

At the hospital, we conferred with her doctor at her bedside. Glynis was game to go on, but the doctor warned that if she did not stay off the foot for at least a week, she ran the risk of permanent impairment. So, despite Glynis's protestations, I decided we would postpone the opening for a week. Having made the decision and mentally accepted the consequences, Jerry and I went to the theatre.

It was now after six o'clock, and a smattering of glittering guests, all in formal attire, had arrived and were milling about in the lobby. I resignedly made the announcement about Glynis and the evening's cancellation, and opened the box office for re-bookings or refunds, and threw open the bars for free drinks. The evening proved, however, a huge disappointment. Many had come from long distances and could not return for the postponed opening.

One such celebrity was Rick Hobard, a fellow producer from New York, who had flown in for the performance. Rick had recently produced a gay-themed play on Broadway that won a Tony award for its leading man, Michael Moriarity. With a European and Middle Eastern background, Rick had a continental manner, with accent to match, that was suave and intriguing. We had met in New York through mutual friends, and have remained good friends to this very day.

Jerry Wayne and I invited the cast, crew and some friends back to our flat for drinks and commiseration, and tried to make the best of a bad situation. Yet, every cloud has a silver lining, and the next day our cancellation made front-page news in every London newspaper!

Everyone suddenly knew we were here, and ticket sales jumped.

The week's wait was agonizing, but it passed. Glynis's foot and shoulder were pronounced healed. Peter Coe wisely eliminated the footboard leap, and we finally had our opening. Now we had only to wait for the reviews.

During intermission, one of our office staff overheard one critic say to another, "Why do the Americans keep mucking about with our British history?" Oh-oh, I thought. That did not augur well. Had we ruffled their feathers just a bit too much with our spoof?

We soon found out: There were about eight London dailies, and most of the reviews were, if not raves, at least decent. The two most influential ones were downright pans—the same two critics that our staff had overheard during intermission! To say that I felt disappointed was putting it mildly.

It was now after midnight, and a typical London drizzle had begun to wet the streets. I walked alone for some time, eventually ducking into an all-night cinema to stare at a screen in thought. Whatever was projected on it made no lasting impression whatsoever. When I emerged, it was daylight and London was awakening.

Walking back to my flat took me past the Garrick Theatre, where our show was playing. My heart quickened when I noticed a line at the box office! Not a long one, but a line, nevertheless, well before the box office was scheduled to open. I sighed the biggest sigh of relief of my life!

We played to decent-sized audiences during the week, and sold out every weekend night. The revenue was enough to keep the show running, but not enough to build up any monetary reserves.

I also had to face the prospect of Glynis leaving. She had signed up for just six months, and as that deadline approached I entreated her to stay on. She was adamant, however, about leaving as planned.

Now I faced a dilemma: If audiences were coming primarily to see Glynis, her replacement would have to be another box office name. If, on the other hand, they were coming because of Keith or the play itself, we might get by with a lesser name. Therefore, we devised a short questionnaire designed to answer that question, and set about canvassing our audience.

Six of us stationed ourselves, one at the head of each of the six aisles, and handed out the questionnaire and a small pencil as each audience member arrived, with the request that they check appropriate boxes and return the questionnaire to an usher during intermission.

Here is where my favorite British anecdote occurred: A tall, buxom, English dowager-type approached me, and I started to give her my pitch. She peered at me through half-lowered lids as I spoke, waited a few beats, and then exclaimed, "WHY are you American?" —pronouncing it "*Amed*ican." The perfect retort came instantly, instead of hours later as it usually does. I looked her directly in the eyes and replied, "Accident of birth, Madam." She held my gaze for a few moments, then uttered, "Pity!" and moved on. I swear, it really happened!

Glynis, indeed, proved to be the draw and I was unsuccessful in finding a name replacement in time, so we closed the show the day she left.

Pity!

TED

During the run of "The King's Mare," I divided my time between London and New York, with occasional trips to the West coast to see Barbara and son Michael. Now that the play had closed, I felt free to spend more time in New York. Jerry Wayne stayed on at the London flat to pursue his—now our—proposed production of the musical, "Two Cities."

In New York one night, a friend invited me to attend a party being given by an acquaintance of his. I rarely say no to a social invitation, so on the appointed evening I joined the party of mixed gay and straight couples and singles. The straight couples were dancing in the living room to recorded music. I tried to mingle, but I have always been uncomfortable with "small talk"—I tend to react rather than instigate—a passive role, I agree, but that's how I am most of the time.

However, this time I found my attention riveted on a tall, slender, black man who stood talking quietly to another man. He wasn't really black-black, but more of a luscious milk chocolate color. I had never met him, but my gaze kept coming back to him over and over. He was immensely attractive, and I became quickly aware of a "something special" feeling inside. Corralling the host, I inquired about his guest's identity. He informed me that the man's name was Ted Ingram, and that Ted lived with a lover who was not present because they were in the throes of breaking up.

I tend to be passive, yes, but on occasion, when sufficiently motivated, I *can* act, and I barged my way into their conversation. The other fellow soon drifted away under the sheer force of my attention to Ted.

Ted and I conversed politely for a while, then I offered, "I dare you to dance with me," whereupon, he took me in his arms and we joined the other dancing couples.

It was…heavenly! *Oh-oh, I thought. Here I go again. Slow down, Stanley, and take it easy!* but I ended up giving Ted my phone number, trying to sound casual while suggesting he call me. He seemed receptive to my attentions, but gave little clue as to his actual interest. Soon after, I left the party and went home.

It was now 2 a.m. My flat mate, Donald Pippin, had retired to his bedroom. In my keyed-up state, sleep, I discovered, was impossible. I sat at my window staring out at the rooftops of New York for hours, thinking of Ted, willing him to call.

Three interminably long days went by, and then my prayers were answered! We arranged to meet for dinner the coming weekend. Neither of us resisted the mutual attraction we felt at dinner, and we began dating on a frequent basis.

We could meet only on weekends because Ted was working two jobs during the week. From 8 a.m. to 4 p.m., he worked as a cloth cutter at a clothing factory, and then hurried to his second job, as a keypunch operator at a computing office, from 5 to 10 p.m. It was a grueling schedule, but Ted was ambitious and eager to improve himself.

As far as I knew, Ted had few black friends...he worked and socialized in a white world. He did, however, have an extended black family, whom I eventually came to know and enjoy. So, conversely, there were occasions

155

when mine was the only white face in a crowd of black ones.

Mingling with all-black groups was eye-opening for me, and I began to visualize what someone like Ted had to deal with in the all-white world he encountered at work and play in Manhattan. He certainly carried it off with ease and aplomb, and with apparent color-blindness. In time, I learned this trait from him, and if not entirely oblivious to color, at least I became comfortable being the only white in a group of blacks. And everyone in Ted's family was warm and welcoming to me. I assumed from the start that they knew and accepted that Ted and I were lovers.

I did discover, however, that among his younger nieces and nephews, an abiding resentment at being discriminated against all their lives lurked just under the surface. I saw a manifestation of this one day when, apparently forgetting about my presence, one of them made a caustic remark about "Whitey." I understood and sympathized with their frustrations about the heavy extra burden of discrimination they carried around, so I said nothing. But one, suddenly remembering my presence, hastened to add, "Of course, we don't mean you...you're different." Now where had I heard that before? Shades of "Goddamn Jew!"

Ted was raised in a small mining town in West Virginia. Apparently his father absented himself early on, and Ted's mother died at an early age, so Ted was brought up by his Aunt Bertha and her husband, Bill, two lovely, gentle people who, though poor, had solid middle class values they imparted to Ted. This upbringing left him with a puritanical streak—despite being gay! For example, some years later, when my son Michael and his girlfriend stayed with us *en route* to a European jaunt, Ted was adamant that the two could not share the same bedroom. And pot smoking was absolutely forbidden. I liked that trait in Ted.

We visited Aunt Bertha and Uncle Bill several times at their home in the Carolinas, and at their later home in Queens, New York. The two graciously accepted our relationship without objection or comment. Ted had a sister, Marie, who, along with husband and children, also lived in Queens. She was a wonderfully supportive person and I became very fond of her. All of Ted's family were good-looking, although to me Ted was the most handsome. Or was I prejudiced?

Ted and I continued to date and...but I'm getting

ahead of myself.

An early morning phone call from Jerry Wayne brought the exciting news that Laurence Harvey had tentatively agreed to play the leading role in the upcoming "Two Cities" musical production!

He wanted, however, to meet the producers before committing. Jerry had set up a breakfast meeting two days hence at the Grosvenor House hotel in London, where Harvey maintained living quarters. So after a hasty phone call to Ted, I packed a bag and flew to London. Laurence Harvey, at that moment, was a big film star and his name would open many doors, including financial ones.

The tabloids had been filled in recent years with Harvey's amorous exploits with various women. Private sources hinted at sexual activities with men, as well. A handsome, dashing figure of a man, he was someone I was looking forward to meeting.

At breakfast, he was warm and charming, talking with enthusiasm about the musical. We had finished eating and were lingering over coffee, when I excused myself to go to the men's room, leaving Jerry and Harvey at the table.

At that hour, the men's room was deserted. I chose the middle of a long line of urinals, and proceeded to relieve myself. Then, in the corner of my eye, I noticed someone approaching me. It was Harvey.

Ignoring all of the other urinals, he chose the one beside me, unzipped his fly and began, I assumed, to relieve himself. Suddenly, with an exaggerated head movement, he leaned over to look at my still-exposed penis. Now, I am not at all ashamed of its size when aroused, but in its resting state, as it was then, my member appears somewhat smaller than average. Having satisfied his curiosity, Harvey zipped up and returned to the table. All this time not a word was spoken.

While we finished our coffee, Harvey politely informed us he was off to do a film in Europe and would be in touch when he returned, but I knew in my heart the deal was off. And I was right. Not long after, his agent informed us that scheduling conflicts had arisen, then that something else interfered, blah-blah-blah, and we should look elsewhere for our leading man.

I never mentioned to Jerry my suspected reason for Harvey's defection, but I knew from experience that on just such momentous and meaningful moments big deals are made and lost!

A year later, Laurence Harvey attended a party in the New York apartment of director Morton DaCosta of "Music Man" fame. DaCosta was a close friend of mine, and I had related my London experience with Lawrence Harvey to him. Putting on his most innocent face, DaCosta casually asked Harvey, "What ever happened to that 'Two Cities' musical I heard you were going to do in London?"

"Oh, I didn't care for the producer," was his answer.

"That's odd. I know him well, and he's a nice fellow."

Harvey simply shrugged and moved away. Ah, show business!

With Harvey gone, my thoughts turned to Keith Michell. His name might not attract large investors, but he was known and admired by London theatre goers, and he had been hugely successful in the musical staging of "The Barretts of Wimpole Street," prior to his "King's Mare" stint.

Keith immediately accepted, and we proceeded to engage the services of an eminent director, Michael Benthall. Now all we needed was the money to bring it all to fruition. I was not in a position at this time to supply the large sum needed. While Jerry got to work on that task, I returned to New York, to my darling Ted.

On my return to New York, Ted and I resumed our dating, until one night he suddenly burst into tears and uttered, with an anguished cry, "I can't keep doing this! It's tearing me apart!"

I knew what was eating at him, for I felt it, too. "It's time to make the choice, Ted."

"I've already made my choice. I want to live together with you," he said, looking at me with apprehension. I knew he was waiting for my reaction, and I was torn. This was what I wanted, with all my heart, but my small, inner voice warned to approach my decision more rationally.

Ted was still living with his (ex?) lover, and if he simply jumped from one bed to the other, I would be placing myself in the role of a home-wrecker. I didn't want "love on the rebound," which might, as often happens, prove short-lived on his part. So I curbed my elation.

"I love you, Ted," I replied cautiously. "And I want us to be together. But I can't do it this way. You have to move out and be on your own. Even then, I think we should move slowly. I don't want either of us to make a hasty decision and risk recriminations. The question is, can we do it my way?"

I watched him silently calm himself. Although he nodded in acknowledgment, I couldn't be certain if he was acknowledging his feelings or agreeing with me, but I didn't press.

After our talk, for a while at least, everything remained status quo.

In the meantime, Donald Pippin, my roommate, informed me that the stage and screen actress, Celeste Holm, had invited both of us to dinner the following week, and he had tentatively accepted for both of us. They knew each other, but I had never met her, so I wondered why I was being included in the invitation.

The reason became apparent when, after cocktails and a lovely dinner at her apartment, Celeste began talking about a fund-raising event she was chairing for a charity organization at Lincoln Center. Would Donald act as musical director and conductor, and would I act as producer in putting the show together? All *gratis*, naturally.

Donald begged off, rightly claiming that his schedule conducting "Mame" would not permit it, but I was intrigued. I agreed to produce it on condition that Celeste would find a "backup" for me should my London activities take me away. She agreed, and I went to work lining up personalities to perform (also *gratis*) for the event.

It was interesting to see who was willing to make the effort for a worthy cause, and who couldn't be bothered.

The musical comedy star, Gwen Verdon, was a love. She took it upon herself to rehearse a dance number with a group of under-privileged children living in a squalid area near Lincoln Center. The evening's charity was to benefit those very kids.

Ballet dancers Edward Villela and Suzanne Farrell agreed to work up a dance duet. Opera star Ezio Pinza gladly accepted. Other celebrity performers of the day quickly came on board, and in no time, our time slots were full! The well-known stars, Helen Hayes and Alan Arkin, agreed to M.C. the show and introduce each act. It would be a stellar evening, with a black-tie audience paying big bucks to benefit the charity.

All involved were consummate professionals, so the run-through, two hours before the performance, went smoothly, including making a grand piano rise from the basement to stage level.

The actual performance also went as planned until—

as the piano slowly ascended on its riser—a disheveled stagehand appeared, standing in front of the piano with a surprised look on his face as he gazed out at the sea of inquisitive faces spread out before him. Guess who got the biggest hand of the evening as he scampered, red-faced, into the wings?

The benefit over, it was time for me to fly back to London and "Two Cities." Jerry had not been successful getting the necessary financial pledges. In fact, it was looking like financing was going to prove a long and difficult task.

I immediately thought of Clem Stone, my "Riot Act" associate producer. This might be just the kind of project that would appeal to him, so I placed the call, and left my message with one of his many secretaries. Within hours he returned the call. "Clem, how would you like to be sole backer and full co-producer of a London musical production of 'A Tale Of Two Cities'?"

"Sounds good. Send me the budget and the script," he returned. Which I did immediately, along with a recording of some of the songs. Three days later, he telephoned: "Count me in! I'll have my people send you the papers. A deal's a deal!"

Jerry and I were giddy with excitement. It was now full steam ahead, and we began setting up auditions, engaging a rehearsal space—in short, preparing to set in motion the myriad tasks necessary to bring "Two Cities" to fruition.

Then the "papers" arrived. I had not been concerned, as Clem was no novice to the customary financial setup of a stage production. Investors get all the profits until the investment is fully recouped. Thereafter, profits are split evenly between investors and producers. So Clem would, after recouping his investment from first profits, receive 50% of subsequent profits as the investor, plus 25% (half the producer's share) as a co-producer, for a total of 75% of profits after payback. It was a shock, therefore, to discover that his lawyers had drawn up the documents to give Clem 100% of everything, with only a modest "office fee" for Jerry and me. It's obviously a mistake, I assured Jerry, and then myself.

Composing a letter of correction, with a copy to Clem, I sent everything back to the attorneys in Chicago. As a safety precaution, I placed a temporary hold on all activities.

A week went by, then two, with no word from Chicago. I placed a call to Clem, but it was not returned.

What had gone wrong? Surely Clem would not insist on those onerous terms. Something strange was going on. Then I thought of Clem's Republican connections and Jerry's rumored blacklist background. Could that be the stumbling block? I decided to address both issues in a telegram to Clem.

"On the basis of 'a deal's a deal,' I bought out my partner, so it will be just you and I as producers. If your lawyers want to change the usual percentages, I am open to discussion. Please advise." Jerry had, in fact, agreed to bow out, with my promise to somehow compensate him if the show succeeded.

Clem never replied. All my efforts to telephone him failed to elicit a callback. I had, over time, become friendly with Clem's publicity agent in New York, and I appealed to her to find out what was wrong. She reported back to me that, when she queried Clem about it, all he would say was, "Yes, that's a shame," and nothing more. To this day, what went wrong remains a mystery.

Jerry and I were once again back to square one, and I was becoming disheartened. I missed Ted, fiercely. The pre-paid lease on the Ivor Novello London suite still had two more months to go, so I told Jerry he could stay on for the two months, but then he would be on his own. I was feeling the need to abandon ship. Back I went to New York.

My Two Wives and Three Husbands

SOMETHING ABOUT ANNE

To my delight, Ted had left his former lover and taken up residence alone in a tiny apartment in Greenwich Village. He was still working two jobs, so we still only met on weekends. Ted lost weight and was beginning to look too thin to me. Then one day, he experienced extreme fatigue and I insisted he consult my doctor, who had the unfortunate name of Hertz (say it aloud). Dr. Hertz was a German refugee, of the old school, who used say to me, "You'll get better with me or without me, but with me, it won't take as long." I was especially appreciative of his frank wisdom.

He needed only a short session with Ted to inform us that Ted was suffering from malnutrition.

Malnutrition! In this day and age? Ted's frantic schedule was playing havoc with his eating, and this was the result. The two-job routine could not continue. Even so, Ted was proud, and would not accept financial help from me. Something had to be done to mitigate his work schedule, and besides, I ached to have him with me every night.

So I hatched a plot.

I knew an optician who had a small but growing optical shop in midtown Manhattan, and I proposed a deal to him. If he would take Ted on as an apprentice and teach him to be an optical lab technician, Ted would work free for three months. My friend agreed. Now I had to convince Ted.

"Move in with me," I said. "I'll support you for those three months, after which you'll be able to get a job in any optical store in town and make more money at one job than you are now earning with two." He didn't even hesitate. Love is a powerful catalyst, and besides, it made sense.

So now instead of cutting cloth, Ted was cutting glass. Not the same thing, of course, but Ted proved a fast learner. My optician friend was so pleased that when the three months ended, he offered to keep Ted on at a very good wage. It helped that Ted was so personable.

Everyone liked him.

I must say, we made a dashing couple. Others said so, too. Freed from the awful two-job burden, Ted blossomed. He was full of élan and enthusiasm. I couldn't help but smile in his presence.

Donald Pippin had no problem with Ted moving in with me, but the lease was due to expire soon and the new rent was exorbitant, so Ted and I looked around for new quarters just for us. We found an ideal apartment in a rent-controlled building at the corner of Central Park West and 64th Street. The living room was even large enough to accommodate the baby grand piano I had bought, in expectation of taking piano lessons. I did take a few lessons, but quickly gave it up. The neglected piano, however, came in handy later on.

Ted and I were sublimely happy. I had no compunction in providing us both a lifestyle that Ted could not otherwise have afforded. We committed to each other, and in our eyes we were "married," just as Emmett and I had been, despite not being recognized as such by church or state. If one of us had more money than the other, so what? It felt no different to me than a legal heterosexual marriage.

At the same time, Anita Loos and I continued talks

about making her play, "The King's Mare," into a musical, and finally decided to hire a composer and lyricist to do the score. The first to vie for the job was Ralph Blane, who, with partner Hugh Martin, had done scores for stage ("Best Foot Forward") as well as screen ("Meet Me In St. Louis"). They had recently decided to go separate ways, and Ralph Blane now had a new writing partner named Jim Gregory. By coincidence, I had met Greg before and liked him. Ralph and Greg volunteered to do some songs "on spec," to which Anita and I agreed.

One week later, they auditioned three songs for us. We were instantly hooked! The numbers had wit, humor and charm. Anita set to work adapting her play into a musical (being no novice, as she had done the same for her play, "Gigi," when it was made into a movie musical). The boys continued with developing the music and lyrics for the production. I was still worried about the weak second act, but Ralph was confident that the problem would resolve musically.

This is where my baby grand piano earned its keep: When we felt the material was ready to be heard, Ralph and Greg prepared to play and sing the entire score for a first batch of potential backers, in my—and Ted's—living room. We had re-named our show "Something About Anne." I had informed Ralph and Greg that many, many more backers' auditions were likely in store, and was satisfied when I heard that the two were game.

When the first audition came up, I asked Ted to absent himself for that part of the evening. I didn't want to take the chance of alienating any potential investors by flaunting my homosexuality.

Ted acquiesced with his usual good nature, but as I thought about it, I began to wonder if it was only the gay issue. Was it also a color issue? Was I being unconsciously guilty of racism? The thought made me blush with shame. Even if it was only the gay angle, what kind of twisted values was I espousing? How dare I subject Ted, my admitted spouse, to any kind of such "back of the bus" treatment? Ted was more important to me than any investor—or any show. From that day on, Ted was by my side at every audition.

In fact, I needn't have worried at all, as Ted's ebullient presence quickly proved an asset. Still, I thank God that I thought things through and recognized for myself the error of my original attitude! It still shames me to think about it.

We didn't seem to be making much headway with attracting a star or finding significant financial support. However, opera director Frank Corsaro became interested in our project. Through Corsaro, Beverly Sills, of the New York City Opera, began to toy with the idea of playing "Anne."

At one of our meetings, I mentioned that I would be hearing Beverly at the opera that evening, where she would be doing "Manon." She asked me where I would be sitting, and I gave her a general direction. "I'll send a few extra 'bumps' in your direction," she chuckled (her role as the madcap heroine,"Manon," involved a scene where she danced, cavorted and "bumped" outrageously). Sure enough, that evening she turned in my direction and bumped me three times!

Sills' nickname, "Bubbles," fit her personality perfectly, and it also fit our Anne of Cleves. My hopes were high, but, alas, in the end she decided that doing eight performances a week in our show would be taking too much of a risk with her voice. Pity!

Summer was fast approaching, and I received a call from Barbara, saying she was planning a month-long trip to Europe with a girlfriend. She wanted to leave Michael in New Jersey with her first cousin, Elise Asch, a divorcee who had a son and daughter close to Michael's age. That was fine with me. With Elise's home just across the river, I could see him often, and that is how I came to meet Elise, whose down-to-earth wisdom deeply impressed me.

She was eight years younger than Barbara, with good-looking features and long black hair that cascaded down her back over the peasant-type blouses and skirts she favored.

Michael had grown into a tall, handsome teenager. He readily accepted the fact that I shared my apartment with a "friend," though as far as I could tell, he had no inkling as to our true relationship. I thanked my lucky stars—and Barbara—for never denigrating me before Michael, but instead, lauding me to the sky.

The month went by all too quickly. Barbara was sailing back from Europe, and her ship was due to dock in New York in a few days. Elise called to say that she planned to be at the pier to greet Barbara, and would I like to join her? Michael and Elise's kids would be busy elsewhere that day.

I agreed. On the appointed day, we were both standing at the dock, watching expectantly as Barbara's ship approached. Elise said something I didn't quite catch, but I thought I heard the word "help."

"What did you say?" I asked, turning to face her.

"I said, I know you are gay, and so am I. Could you help me meet some gay women?" At that time the word "lesbian" was not yet in fashion.

"Of course!" I exclaimed and hugged her. "Ted and I know a lot of gay girls in New York. We'd be happy to introduce you to them."

In the course of the next few months, Ted and I introduced Elise to at least twenty "available" gay women. She had one-time dates with many, but to no avail. None of them appealed emotionally to her.

"For Heaven's sake, Elise, what kind of woman are you looking for?" I asked, and she promptly provided me a rundown of the qualities she was looking for in a mate. I listened, mesmerized.

"Oddly," I replied, "you have just described someone I know in California. Her name is Aviva and she is gay, but she already has a mate and isn't available." So much for that...or so I thought.

Not long after our talk, on June 29, 1969—I will always remember the day—many newspapers ran headlines about a gay bar called Stonewall, in Greenwich Village, that had been raided the previous night by the vice squad and, for the first time ever, gay patrons fought back. Protests turned into riots. Most people today mark the event as the beginning of the gay pride movement. Actually, a few gay organizations already existed: the Mattachine Society for gay men, the Daughters of Bilitis for gay women. But these were quiet, unassuming groups, mainly providing meeting places for information dissemination and discussions. Stonewall was different. This was in-your-face live action. This was a national "coming out of the closet," and the door was never to be shut again!

Straight society seemed horrified, though frightened may be more accurate, and the old taboos remained firmly in place. Perhaps not as firmly as before, but they were still there. Homosexuality was then thought by most straight people to be a deliberate choice. Gays, of course, knew that this was not true. Much later, medical science would catch up and prove the "choice" notion false. My retort to that British dowager comes to mind: "Accident of birth, Madam!" Even back then, a modicum of common sense should have made it clear that no person would willingly choose the life of fear and intimidation that came with it. At the same time, few of us could imagine the huge forward strides that gays would make in the years to come.

Meanwhile, backers' auditions continued for "Something About Anne." I had sent a script, through her agent, to Leslie Caron, the dancing gamin with whom I had gone grunion hunting in Malibu so long ago, and her agent called to say Caron liked the script, was interested, and wanted to hear the score before deciding. I wasted no time in sending a recording of the score. Since everyone who heard it agreed that it was excellent, I had high hopes and proceeded to impart the good news to Anita Loos.

To my astonishment, Anita retorted, "Over my dead body!" and refused to discuss it further. Investigation revealed that the two had gone through a serious and protracted argument of some kind during the shooting of the film "Gigi," for which Anita had adapted her play of the same name. Apparently Caron no longer harbored any ill will, but Anita still carried a grudge. Well, I thought, if Caron says "Yes," we'd simply have to find a way of smoothing Anita's ruffled feathers.

The issue, however, became moot when Caron's

agent reported that she did not like the score, and was turning us down. I've always wondered if Anita's opposition somehow got back to Caron. In the meantime, auditions continued!

One day, I read in the trade papers that Rex Harrison was in New York. Remembering that Hanya Holm had choreographed "My Fair Lady," which starred Harrison, I prevailed upon Selma Tamber, my new office-mate, to ask her client if she would bring him to an audition. Selma agreed to try. Sure enough, on the appointed evening, Selma and Hanya appeared with Rex Harrison and his wife, the British actress, Rachel Roberts.

The presentation went exceptionally well, I thought, with Greg at the piano and Ralph singing his heart out. At the end, Hanya turned to Harrison and said, "I'll do the choreography if you agree to do the show." My heart leaped into my throat as we awaited Rex's reply.

"I like it," he replied, "but I don't want to undertake any more leading roles on stage." My heart faltered. "However," he went on, "I would be interested in directing it, and I think Rachel," he pointed to his wife, "would make a great Anne."

This time, my heart threatened to leap out of my throat. With Rex Harrison directing, every door would open. I tried to hide my excitement, as we arranged for Rex and Rachel to return the following day so that Rachel could sing for us—I had seen Rachel Roberts in films and knew she was a talented actress, but had no idea if she could sing.

The next day, Rachel surprised us by having a strong, beautiful, singing voice. They were leaving for London the following day, so I gathered up all the material I had on hand, mainly the script and sheet music for the score, and packaged it for Rex to take with him. He promised to study the material and get back to us soon.

Ralph, Greg and I were ecstatic. As soon as Harrison agreed to direct it, we could announce his participation and roll into action. Does this remind you of anything? Wise Anita was not so sanguine. She had by now been through too many show business ups and downs. "We'll see," was all she would offer.

Not two weeks later, the papers everywhere were shouting the news that Rex Harrison and Rachel Roberts were divorcing! Ouch! Maybe that meant she was out, but he was still in? I decided to wait a decent period to allow the dust to settle, and then contact Rex directly, which I did, or more correctly tried to do. His agents informed me that he was in Portofino and was unreachable. When would he return? No one knew. Could a message be sent to him? No, he had given strict orders to that effect.

All we could do was wait. And so we waited. And waited. Then an article appeared in the trade papers mentioning that Rex Harrison was cruising aboard the yacht of his good friend, Leslie Bricusse, a British composer who had written numerous hit shows for stage and film. So, Harrison had not yet returned to London after all. Three weeks later, the same trade papers reported that Leslie Bricusse was preparing a musical based on Henry the Eighth!

I was livid. I'd heard that Harrison could be difficult and even nasty in his dealings, but it was the feeling of being stabbed in the back that hurt most. Public knowledge that someone of Bricusse's clout was preparing a musical similar to ours would be a death knell to potential investors for us. Disgusted, disheartened, dejected, I threw in the towel.

At least I was lucky in love. Bloodied and bowed (and getting increasingly lower on funds), I decided to give up Broadway and show business. It had been a heady ride, with many thrills and disappointments. I regretted none of it, but realized that show business had become an all-too-demanding mistress. I was determined to free myself from the enticing enslavement and focus on what was truly meaningful and precious to me: my love for Ted.

I told Ted I needed to pull up stakes and move back to sunny California, where I could return to what I knew best—the optical business—especially now that Ted was a lab technician. We could work together at one of my offices! Ted was game, so the decision was made.

My producer friend, Rick Hobard, assumed the lease on my New York office space.

Wanting to maintain our rent-controlled apartment on Central Park West, I sub-leased it, fully furnished, to a doctor and his young "friend." Then I bought a previously-owned station wagon, and Ted and I began our preparations to leave New York and drive to California and a new life together.

THE WESTWARD TREK

Ted and I had the choice of two routes West: one to the North, which ran the risk of snowstorms; and one to the South, which, while more desirable weather-wise, might prove dicey prejudice-wise, as Ted and I planned to stop regularly at dine-in restaurants and, evenings, stay in motels. It was early November of 1972. Racial inter-marriage, which had been staunchly banned in many states, was suddenly legal throughout the country, thanks to the U.S. Supreme Court. Racial prejudice still flourished in the deep South, though subdued in the northern states.

When I was stationed in Florida during World War II, signs were posted all over that read "Restricted Clientele," local code for "no Jews or blacks." Those signs gradually disappeared after the war, but I feared that some southerners might still maintain that attitude, or worse, be looking for a situation in which they could demonstrate their abhorrence to these new liberties. In the end, weather concerns won out, and bravely—or stupidly —we decided to throw our caution regarding the southern route to the wind. So there we were, a Jew and a black homosexual couple, invading new territory in every sense of the phrase.

Our first stop, however, was Philadelphia, to see my parents. I had called ahead and my folks had prepared lunch for my "roommate" and me. They knew I shared my apartment with a male friend, but knew nothing else about Ted.

There is no one, in my experience, more prejudiced against a minority than another minority, and I had often heard my parents denigrate the "shvartzes" (Yiddish for blacks). So I was more than a little apprehensive as we arrived. On the other hand, it had been my decision to stop by with Ted. Was I flinging down the gauntlet to my family, challenging them with the dual taboos of sexual and racial discriminations? Or was I testing myself? Whatever my subconscious motivation, I was tense and nervous about the coming visit. At the same time, I tried not to transmit my feelings to Ted, hoping his usual self-confidence and charm would carry the day, which, in fact, proved to be the case.

My widowed sister, Anna, was on hand, along with my parents, and everyone, to my relief, was warm and welcoming. After lunch, we sat and talked. Ted, Anna and Pop sat on one side of the room, while Mom and I quietly spoke on the other side.

At one point, my mother said, with a toss of her head in Ted's direction, "He's Italian?"

"No," I said, and went on with our conversation.

We talked about three minutes more, then, with another toss of her head, "He's Spanish?"

"No," I replied and again resumed our previous discussion.

This time she waited almost five minutes. Another toss of the head, "He's a schvartzer?"

"Yes," I said, and went on with our discourse.

She said nothing further on the subject until, as we bid our farewells, she threw her arms around Ted and exclaimed, "You're such a nice boy...and you're so lucky to have my son as your friend!" I wasn't at all sure how to take that, so I simply said goodbye and we left.

Did she know? Coming from the old country, poorly

educated and totally unsophisticated, surely they were not "hip." But *did* she know at some level? Offspring tend to under-estimate their parents. At any rate, I never told them any more about our relationship and they never asked further.

I do know, however, that I had initially created a wall between myself and my family. That, of course, was the need to hide my "secret." Later, after I "came out" to my family, that wall vanished entirely and I was able to relate to them with ease. That coming out, related later, occurred after both of my parents had died, so I'm left to wonder if my mother and father could have—and would have—tried to understand. I like to think so, and now I'm sorry I kept that wall in place between them and me all those years.

Afterward, when Ted and I discussed the visit, we agreed that she probably was not aware of our love-relationship, but was referring to the white-black issue. "Did that bother you?" I asked. His answer was revealing. "No more than what I have to deal with all the time." So his skin was not as thick as he pretended. My heart went out to him; I just wanted to envelop him in love, to protect him from the slings and arrows of racial discrimination.

We settled in for our drive through the South, through Georgia, Alabama and Mississippi. What would we encounter? Looking back, I sincerely believe that the TV series, "I Spy," with the white/black team of Robert Culp and Bill Cosby that had been successfully running and had proven so popular nationwide, helped prepare the way a great deal for us. Also, Ted had an air of assurance about him that gave the impression that he owned the world. Plus, as I said before, we *were* a dashing couple! I suspect that strangers, seeing us together, assumed we were "celebrities"—entertainers or athletes. We encountered no hostilities, no "incidents."

In California, we had pre-booked a small hotel in Hermosa Beach, a little community south of Los Angeles, for our arrival. After more than a week of driving, we pulled up to the hotel entrance just as our car died. Our engine simply gave out.

It was evening, so we decided to wait until the next morning to call the Auto Club and have the car towed in for repairs, considering it a good omen that the engine had waited until we arrived before giving up the ghost; a fitting comment on our old life left behind, and our new one dawning.

Several days later, we found and rented a small but attractive "adobe hut" residence near the beach and moved in. My only personal friend in the area was Aviva Kamin—she whom Barbara's cousin, Elise, had unwittingly described to me. Aviva and her lover, Mary, were a big help to us getting settled, and introduced us to their many friends.

One of my optometry offices was in near-by Torrance, so that's where Ted went to work. Optometry law in California had been amended, during my absence, to prevent any optometrist from owning more than two offices, but my existing four offices had been "grandfathered" in.

Dick Mast had been supervising them and they were doing well. Occasionally, Dick would visit the Torrance office, where Ted was working in the lab. Dick had a compulsion to tell others how they should be doing their jobs, and he proceeded one day to tell Ted how he should more properly hold a lens he was grinding.

Now, Ted had one exception to his usual affability: He didn't suffer fools gladly, and he could be very vocal when he disapproved. On this occasion, he barked at Dick, "Don't tell me how to do my job. Get out of here!"

Dick, the tiger, reverted immediately to the chastened pussycat, treating Ted with kid gloves thereafter.

Which reminds me of another time when Ted told somebody off. It was at a party at our house. A friend—Helen—had recently had a facelift. She was prone to histrionics, and when Ted gave her the typical Southern California "hello" kiss on her cheek, she reared back in dramatic anguish.

"Don't touch my face!" she wailed. Ted thrust an arm toward her, forefinger extended, and shouted, "Helen! If you can't take that face out in public, leave it home!" Even Helen had to laugh.

Our adobe hut was charming, but quickly proved too tiny for us and our rapidly growing social circle. It was time to move to bigger quarters.

I wanted to live closer to Hollywood, where more of my re-emerging friends lived. Even though it meant a longer commute for Ted, we found and bought a modest two-bedroom house with a great canyon view, close to Mulholland Drive, north of Hollywood and Beverly Hills.

Early one morning, a phone call came with the news that the doctor to whom we had rented our New York apartment had committed suicide by setting fire to the apartment. His friend was unharmed, but everything in the apartment was a total loss with the exception of the grand piano, which miraculously escaped major damage. So I had the piano shipped to our house in the hills and gave up the apartment in New York. Was the world going crazy, with even doctors committing suicide?

We lived on Carmar Drive, and quickly met two lesbians who lived on the same street. We all liked each other and soon were spending time at each other's homes. One night, the girls were at our house for dinner when the phone rang. I answered.

It was Radie Harris, a columnist for the *Hollywood Reporter*, whom I knew from my New York days. I had been one of her "stable" of single (mostly gay) young men whom she could count on to escort her to celebrity functions, where she gathered her material.

"Stanley!" she enthused. "I'm in town and I'd like you to take me to dinner with the Newmans tomorrow night." It so happened, however, that Ted and I had made a date to have dinner tomorrow evening at the ladies' house.

I replied, "You mean dinner with Paul Newman and Joanne Woodward?" My listeners' ears perked up. "Gee,

Radie, I'm awfully sorry, but I already have a previous engagement."

"Oh, Stanley, can't you break it?" everyone heard. Ted and the ladies motioned vigorously for me to accept, so I did, even though the invitation was for me alone.

The following evening, I drove to Beverly Hills where Radie was staying and picked her up. In the car, she proceeded to give me directions. It soon became apparent that we were driving away from the Newmans' home and toward downtown Los Angeles. It turned out that "dinner with the Newmans" was a large banquet at the University of Southern California, honoring Paul Newman. I held my tongue, but was furious...but only until we were seated.

The tables were long and narrow, and as I sat down, I looked across straight into the eyes of Mae West. MAE WEST! Next to meeting Greta Garbo, this was the biggest thrill of my life. She was in the later phase of her career, and though her hair was a bit stringy, she had lost none of her moxie sparkle.

As Radie wandered off seeking tidbits for her column, I had a few minutes to converse with Mae West before the other celebrities, including Paul Newman, came by to kneel at Mae's side and pay homage. She was funny and very naughty, and it was on that occasion that she gave me that line I still use in my own life: "I owe it all to dirty living!" That line never fails to crack people up. Especially me, because it happens to contain more than just a kernel of truth!

It was at about this time that Elise moved to Southern California, just as Aviva and Mary were breaking up. Talk about serendipity! I introduced Elise to Aviva and the rest, as they say, is history. They clicked immediately and are still together as I write, more than forty years later. Among my many admitted attempts at matchmaking, this was my greatest—and only—real success!

When Selma Tamber and I had shared office space in New York, she had asked if her nephew, film producer Martin Poll, could also share our space temporarily while he and his assistant, Gloria Michel, did some pre-production work on Poll's upcoming film "A Lion In Winter." That was okay with me, and that was how I first met another major figure in my "new" life, Gloria Michel.

Gloria was petite, pretty and perky, with dark hair and a trim, shapely figure. Somewhat younger than I, she was a divorcee with grown children. Organized and fearless, she would take on and tackle any task regardless of obstacles. She also knew and appreciated the value of real friendship, and ours still flourishes. Now she was living in Los Angeles, and we gladly renewed our acquaintance.

Another lady I had first met in New York, actress/ singer Evelyn Ward (she pronounced her first name the British way, as EEvelin) was also now in L.A. She was the mother of teenage heartthrob David Cassidy. Most people thought David's mother was Shirley Jones because of the family roles David and Shirley played in "The Partridge Family" on TV, but Shirley was actually David's stepmother, having married Jack Cassidy after he and Evelyn divorced. By the time I met Evelyn in New York, she had re-married a noted film director and re-divorced!

Evelyn was a beautiful, full-figured brunette. I would even call her voluptuous. Her singing voice was glorious, and she often enlivened our California parties with her vocalizing.

A third lady who became a good friend was Nancy Vandis, married to the Greek actor, Titos Vandis, who appeared in both the stage and film versions of "Never

On Sunday."

The word "baby-doll" described Nancy perfectly. Blonde and diminutive, she had a beautiful face and personality to match. She had been in the chorus of the Broadway production of "Never On Sunday," which is where she met Titos Vandis. They later divorced and Nancy's figure changed from petite to full-blown, though she always retained her effervescent spirit.

In subsequent years, these three women, Gloria, Evelyn and Nancy, were to play major roles in my life. I still think of them as my three "muses." Through the years we remained staunch friends, sharing life's joys and sorrows. We knew we could always count on each other in any hour of need. That's real friendship, in my book, and these were real friends.

Interestingly, almost all of my close friends, apart from other gays, were either single women or married couples. I can recall very few single, straight men who were close to me. Was that sexual tension on my part? On their part? I don't know.

So now all three of my muses were living nearby me in Hollywood. One night, Nancy and Titos Vandis came to our house for dinner along with Gloria, Evelyn and some other friends of ours. Titos had mentioned that Melina Mercouri, his co-star in "Never On Sunday," was in town and could he ask her to stop by later in the evening? I assured him that it would be fine.

Later that evening, as we relaxed after dinner, the doorbell rang, and I admitted Melina and an entourage of several fellow-actors. Melina was stunningly charismatic. After initial introductions by Titos, Melina stood for a few moments, silently perusing the room. Her eyes swept from left to right and partway back again, then lighted on Ted, who was sitting on the floor. She obviously liked what she saw because, without a moment's hesitation, she bounded across the room and sat down on the floor next to Ted. *Oh-oh*, I thought, with some trepidation, *This will prove interesting!*

Not to worry. After quickly sorting out the various people and their relationships (Ted's and mine being foremost, given the situation), she settled down to loving our little house and its great view, saying, rather wistfully, "I feel so peaceful here." We invited her to come back anytime she wished, but never saw her again.

About that time, my sister, Anna, telephoned from Philadelphia to ask if she and Mom could come out for a week's visit. My father had died about a year before, and

I had returned to Philadelphia for his funeral. Although I was really fond of my Pop, he had always been a figure in the background of a scene dominated by my mother. And so it was in his death. It was she who needed consoling, she who was to be pitied. All attention, including mine, went mainly to her. *That's a son's job*, I reasoned.

Responding to my sister's call, I assured her we would always have room for them. Ted and I were still "in the closet" to my family, so after our visitors arrived, I told them that they would have Ted's bedroom, while he bunked in with me. "Ted's room," actually the guest room, had one queen-size bed, while "my" (really our) master bedroom boasted a king-size bed.

As I escorted Mom and Anna to their quarters, Mom peeked into "Ted's room," sniffed and said, pointing to the master bedroom, "I'll sleep in there." I was certain I knew what was going through her mind. She didn't want to sleep in the bed where the "shvartzer" slept. Little did she know that, if I had let her have her way, that's exactly where she would have ended up sleeping!

I seldom get angry, but with cold fury, I pointed to the guestroom and pronounced, "These are the arrangements, and *that* is where you will sleep!"

Not used to being thwarted, Mom drew herself up to her full height and huffed, "I'm leaving."

Without a moment's hesitation, I replied, "I'll drive you to the airport." Even as I said it, I couldn't believe the words were coming out of my mouth! Never had I directly defied my mother. Nice Jewish boys simply do not do that. Sure, many times I yessed her, and then did whatever I wanted behind her back, but never in direct defiance!

Taken aback, Mom paused, thought it over, and made her decision: "I'll stay a few days. But I'll sleep on the living room sofa."

"Fine!" I said, and proceeded to make up the sofa for her. As it turned out, Anna was relieved to have "Ted's room" all to her self.

Through all this, Ted remained the silent onlooker. I can only guess what he was thinking and feeling but, as I knew, he had honed his acting skills during a lifetime of slights. To his credit, he was as charming to both Anna and Mom as ever.

The next morning, Mom decided she would, after all, sleep for the rest of the week with Anna in the queen-size bed. To my surprise, it was now Anna's turn to defy

Mom.

"Oh, no you don't!" came Anna's quick reply. "You chose the couch and that's where you'll stay." I guess rebellion is catching! The whole thing proved an entirely new experience for my mother. After a few silent moments, she meekly acquiesced, and on the sofa she slept for the rest of the week. It didn't occur to me at the time, but now I suspect that Anna must have been well aware of Mom's aversion, and was actually assisting me in *my* defiance. To Mom's credit, by the end of that week, she had become genuinely fond of Ted.

On the last day of their visit, we invited some friends to a pool party at our house. One of the guests was Mom's sister, my Aunt Lil, who lived in Los Angeles. Lil was down to earth, unpretentious and plainspoken. At the end of the day's activities, as Lil was saying her goodbyes, she threw her arms around Ted's neck, kissed him on the cheek and proclaimed, "Who could hate you?" Who, indeed! Ted had done it again, peeling away racial prejudice to allow the person to see the individual rather than just the color of his skin.

A small aside: If, at our best, it sounds like we were less than non-discriminatory, then I have succeeded in conveying a faithful reflection of the times. It's easy to imagine the various walls of discrimination as suddenly falling away, when it was, in my experience, more of a slow crumbling, with moments of surprising clarity interspersed with longer periods of no change, resistance and, sometimes, even frank reversion. The same pattern of inevitable but slow acceptance was proceeding for gays.

My Two Wives and Three Husbands

SHERMAN OAKS

Almost by accident, Ted and I learned of city plans to build a dog-exercise park, to be located directly below our house. Ted and I, though dog owners, feared it would be noisy, so we tried to fight it. When the park finally seemed inevitable, we decided to move.

Gloria Michel was now a real estate agent, and she began showing us properties. One Sunday, Ted and I happened to drive by an "open house" in Sherman Oaks —a nice neighborhood in the San Fernando Valley—and went in. The house was *huge*, with many bedrooms, a pool, a guesthouse and large grounds, all gated. It even had a fully stocked bomb shelter built under the large garage! Ted seemed interested. *No way could we afford this*, I thought. *Totally out of our reach.*

The present owners, however, had done a terrible job

of decorating, and it took quite a bit of imagination to see what it *could* look like. So, there had been no offers, and the asking price had begun dropping. We brought Gloria around to see it and she assured us, "The house is structurally sound; it just needs cosmetic work."

The price was still high, and what would we do with all that space? It happened that I had been preparing to sell a small apartment complex I had bought a long time ago under the GI Bill of Rights. The price I contemplated asking was considerably less than the property we were now looking at. So I airily said, "If they'll do an even trade, I'll go for it."

The owners must have been desperate, because they accepted.

Oh-oh! I thought. *Now we had a veritable estate on our hands.* I ended up calling it "Disneyland West." While the Carmar Drive house was on the market, we redecorated the Sherman Oaks place. In the end, it turned out better than we dreamed. We had slowly acquired three standard poodles—the big ones—so the spacious grounds were ideal for their romping; so much so, we eventually ended up with five large poodles!

My son, Michael, in the meantime, had graduated

from San Francisco State College with a degree in accounting, in the process becoming a Haight-Ashbury hippie, long hair and all. I suspected that he was into the drug scene, though when I queried him, he confessed only to use of pot. I had my doubts.

One day he telephoned. "Dad, I'm thinking of trying LSD. What do you think about it?"

My mind went into overdrive. Was my son actually asking my permission? Or was he asking me to forbid it? Or to condone it? Not being sure, I chose a middle route.

"From the little I've read about it, it sounds dangerous. No one knows enough about its long-term effects. So don't do anything yet. Let me do some further research. If it proves harmless, maybe we'll both try it together, but wait until you hear from me about it."

He promised he would. Had I dodged a bullet? Would he really hold off? I never knew, because suddenly —soon after that call—he found religion, cut his hair short and was as square as square could be! Barbara and I were astonished when Michael became a member of what I can only describe as a "cult"...a movement calling itself Christian, but unaffiliated with any mainstream denomination. Michael had a Jewish girlfriend at the time, who ended up calling me in tears because Michael would no longer see her. In fact, his group advised against maintaining any former associations, including family, but Michael didn't go that far, thank goodness.

"Don't worry," I told the girlfriend. "It's just a phase...he'll come out of it."

Never have I been so wrong. I knew that challenging his new-found "religion" would only drive him deeper into it, so I played it cool, maintaining a neutral stance. When he announced he was marrying a girl in the Oregon branch of the same movement, however, I knew it was more than a passing fancy.

Barbara and I flew to Coos Bay, Oregon, for the wedding. I felt like a fish out of water among all the evangelical fundamentalists, but my heart went out to Rhoda, Michael's bride-to-be. As I sat beside her after the ceremony, I felt her trembling and put my arm around her, as I wondered what was frightening her so. I found out later it was merely a young girl's trepidation at facing marriage.

Barbara proved smarter than any of us. She and I both felt in danger of losing our son, so Barbara became a member of his "church." I was unable, or unwilling, to go that far, but remained supportive. My patience, however, was sorely tried when Michael began trying to convert Ted and me. This was too much!

"Michael," I said, "when you were growing up, your mother and I never tried to influence you about religion, right?" He nodded in affirmation. "Then please do me the courtesy of returning the favor."

He looked at me for a moment, and then said, "You're right," and never tried to persuade me or Ted again.

He and Rhoda settled in Berkeley for a time, where their first child, Charles, was born. Then they moved to Colorado, where Rhoda gave birth to a girl, Danielle, then another girl, Ilana. Michael had a good job as a certified public accountant. Ted and I visited them several times, and all was well. They were still steeped in their religion, but were no longer overbearing about it.

Occasionally, they would visit us, staying at our house. I have to laugh every time I recall one such visit. I overheard Charles, then about six or seven, saying to his mother—they were in an adjacent room—"Mom, are Grandpa and Ted married?"

To which Rhoda hastily replied, "Don't be silly...two men can't be married to each other." Now, where had I heard that before? Back came Charles' response, "Well, they sure act like they're married."

Out of the mouths of babes!

The time eventually came when Ted and I decided that Michael and Rhoda had to be told. We were tiring of having to watch our behavior in our own home. So I took it upon myself to tell them on their next visit.

They took the news calmly. Had they known or at least suspected? Later, we were to discover that they had *thought* about the possibility once or twice, but had not formed any conclusion. Anyway, by this time it didn't matter to them, one way or the other. Sure, their religion frowned upon it, but we were family and that had begun to trump all else. Actually, it was easier than any of us imagined at the time! Their children never had to be told…they just knew. Each generation seems more hip than the previous one.

Speaking of "hip," I want to jump ahead some years to when grandson Charles was twenty-four years old. He and I were alone when he said to me, "Grandpa, how do I know I'm not gay?"

"Well," I replied, "if you have to ask that question, then you are not. If you were gay, you would already know it. Besides, you've had girlfriends, and I assume

S. Stanley Gordon

you've had sexual relations with them."

"Yes, I have. But how can I be sure I'm not missing something?" I waited to see what he had in mind.

"I have gay friends, and I'm going to ask one of them to sleep with me." He didn't have to spell out what he meant by "sleep." Watching me, he continued: "Then I'll know for sure."

Wow! I thought. This guy is really secure. "If you do that," I advised, "make sure it is safe sex. And promise me you will report to me afterward." He assured me that he would.

About a week later, he telephoned to say he had "done it."

"So…report."

"It was pleasurable," Charles said, "and I enjoyed it. But it couldn't begin to compare with being with a woman."

"Aha! So now you know for sure you are not gay."

"That's right," he said confidently, adding, "And now, for the first time, I understand how you can be gay, yet still marry a woman and have children. I never understood that before, but now I do."

I never verbalized it to Charles, but I was so proud of his total lack of guile, his forthright, unprejudiced quest to satisfy himself as to his sexual orientation. Not that I am recommending this experiment to other youngsters. In my experience, a person is either gay or not; heart and yearnings always tell in the end. I've known very few people who fall firmly in the middle, and are equally sexually attracted to both males and females.

Now back to my story. For Ted and me, life could not be better. Our social life was filled with friends, old and new. One of the groups that embraced us included Marsha Hunt and husband Robert Presnell, actor Bert Freed and wife Nancy, writer Ernst Jacobi and wife Lenore, retired Universal Studio publicity head Ben Halpern and wife Lois, famous actor Karl Malden and wife Mona. They had all known each other in New York, when young and struggling to "make it" in their respective professions.

Karl Malden was unassuming and knowledgeable on many subjects besides acting, and Mona was fascinating in her own right. She had given up acting when she married Karl, but she has that built-in "star quality" radiance. When she walked into a room, it still lit up, that same quality Garbo had. No doubt in my mind, she could have been a star, but she enjoyed her life as wife to Karl and mother to their children. What could be better than that?

One of my three muses had a friend, the mother of a well-known actress, who joined our group on some occasions. She developed a crush on Ted—which was understandable. Everybody loved Ted. This poor lady drank too much, too often, and when "in her cups," would proceed to proclaim her desire for Ted to anyone within earshot, which included me one day. Suddenly realizing whom she was addressing, she hastened to include me in her desired conquests. For entirely other reasons, she was soon dropped from our group, thank goodness.

Of course, over the years, other straight women were attracted to Ted...as well as to me. My three muses often mused aloud that if Ted and I were straight, the three ladies would have competed among themselves for our affections. But there was never any serious threat to our relationship by anyone, straight or gay. Isn't that what commitment means?

I've forgotten which family affair it was, but about this time, somebody's wedding or bar mitzvah came up in Philadelphia. Ted couldn't be spared from his job at the office, so I flew back alone for the occasion.

When the time approached for me to return to

California, I decided it was also the right moment to let my siblings in on my "secret." My brother, Ben, his wife, Natalie, and my sister, Anna, drove me to the airport. Brother Dave couldn't make it. As Ben, who was driving, pulled into a parking space, I said, "Stay in the car for a few minutes. There is something I want to tell you."

This moment had been rehearsed in my mind several times during the previous twenty-four hours, so I was serene in the knowledge that I could be calm and collected and matter-of-fact in the delivery. To my surprise, I began to sweat profusely and shake. Nevertheless, I plowed ahead.

"The man I'm living with is not just a roommate. We are lovers. I've been homosexual my whole life."

Natalie wordlessly grasped my hand and squeezed it. Ben just smiled. Anna said, "Gee, when you were a kid that was something terrible, but now it's no big deal. I see it on the Phil Donahue television show all the time."

Thank you, Phil Donahue, I thought. Well, I'd done it! It proved more of an ordeal than I had anticipated, but they had come through for me, as I was sure—well, *almost* sure—they would. There had been a previous harbinger of family acceptance when I revealed my secret to my brother, Meyer, and his wife, Marion, so I needn't have worried…but still…

Some years after Meyer died, Marion remarried. She and I had kept in touch through the years. She had been the first straight person to say to me "Gee—what you and Ted have is really a marriage, isn't it? What a shame you can't call it that." Her new husband was a terrific guy whom all of us liked. He was to die prematurely of a heart attack. Poor Marion! Having to bury two husbands! With her second husband, she had produced a son, Eric Bass.

As the years flew by, I learned that Eric had become a Doctor of Optometry (of all things!), was graduating from the optometry college at Berkeley, and had married a fellow graduate, Lori. Although not related to me by blood, in my mind I considered Eric, through Marion, a nephew.

He and Lori visited Ted and me in Sherman Oaks, as they were re-locating from Berkeley to Southern California, and we developed an instant rapport. Neither of them had to be told of the relationship between Ted and me; they recognized it at a glance and it was no big deal.

By coincidence, one of my doctor employees in

Orange County had given notice, and I offered the position to Eric. He accepted, and they bought a house near that office. Eric proved to be a big asset...he was bright, personable, ambitious, and fun to boot. What's more, his patients loved him. Eric called me "Uncle Sam," and looked to me as a mentor. In a classic example of the pupil overtaking his teacher, Eric was to play an ever more important role in my professional life.

Eric had not yet met my son, Michael, who was still working and living in Denver with his family; that meeting was to occur six months later as Michael underwent an unexpected transition.

My son called me to say he had been offered a very lucrative job in Los Angeles. A member of his religious group had started a business and lured Michael to join his firm as an executive, at double the salary he had been making, plus a new Mercedes company car to use as his own. Michael had already accepted the offer, so his call was merely to alert me about their imminent move, and to ask my help in finding suitable living quarters for him and his family.

"How could I turn it down?" he asked, as though apologizing for not asking my advice beforehand. While fiercely proud of making his own decisions, he usually sought my blessing after the fact. So, I agreed, but inwardly thought it was too good to be true. This, I decided, bore close watching.

Gloria, my real-estate-agent muse, Ted and I immediately set about house hunting for the kids and quickly found the perfect one for them: a country-style, three-bedroom home with a big tree, suitable for climbing, a guesthouse in the rear, and room for the children and their dog to romp freely. Best of all, it was in Sherman Oaks, close to Ted and me.

Barbara, who was now living with her mother in San Francisco, wanted to be near the kids, too, and we found a small apartment for her nearby. Barbara's mother, Esther, ended up moving into the kids' guesthouse! For some reason Barbara and her mother wanted to live apart from each other, though close by. I wisely stayed out of that situation!

Now my whole immediate family was near me. Business was good. Ted and I were happy. We had gay friends and straight friends who intermingled comfortably. We loved and were, in turn, loved. It was a glorious time!

The firm Michael now worked for turned out to be a

"boiler room" operation, selling oil and gas drilling lots in Alaska, by phone. Oh-oh! Warning bells clanged, but I kept my misgivings to myself, for the moment. Michael had to learn for himself.

When they offered Michael the presidency of the firm, however, I felt I had to intervene. I told him the whole thing smelled bad. Michael was certain a church friend could do no wrong and turned a deaf ear. Finally, I did secure his promise that he would accept no stock or any kind of ownership position for the time being. When the government took action a year later and shut down the entire operation, Michael was lucky to escape unscathed. His heart bruised, but wiser for the experience, he had to seek other employment.

I had an idea.

JOY AND SORROW

Dick Mast and I had formed a company to, in effect, act as consultants to independent optometrists, and our duties were increasing. My quasi-nephew Eric, having bought one of my offices and then opening a second office, had become one of the doctors in the group for whom Dick and I were providing consultative services. Duties were expanding while Dick and I were getting on in years. Dick had a son, also named Michael (!), who was a computer programmer. *Now might be the time*, I thought, *to bring both our sons into the business and groom them to eventually replace us*. Dick agreed, and both Michaels came to work for us. The process proceeded smoothly, the two getting along well with each other.

Ted and I were now wanting to do more pleasure

travelling, and found ourselves chafing under the restraints of Ted's job. It seemed whenever I wanted us to go away on a vacation on short notice, we couldn't because Ted could not be spared from his duties at the optical office. So I fired him!

We reasoned that Ted could replace me as the "house husband," taking over many of the domestic chores I had been performing. He also became a kind of roving emissary for me, visiting the various offices, reporting problems back to me before they became major ones. But more importantly, we were now free to travel together at will.

As an icing on our happiness cake, Michael and Rhoda presented me with a new granddaughter, Talia.

But something odd seemed to be happening to Ted. We had always enjoyed playing tennis together, but he developed what we thought was a strained muscle in one leg, so we stopped. A trip to China was in the immediate offing, so Ted bought a cane and we went. On the trip, his personality took a turn for the worse. He became cranky, occasionally snapping at me with harsh words. It was totally at odds with his usual sunny disposition.

Obviously, the pain in his leg was getting worse, so

immediately upon our return, I insisted he seek medical help. Tests were done, and back came the preliminary report: CANCER!

At first, the doctor thought it was bone cancer, because in testing his leg they found cancer cells in that bone. This was a hammer blow. I hastened to the UCLA medical library to read up on bone cancer. Not good, but not hopeless. Some bone cancer patients did recover, though the odds were not great. A number of UCLA students, walking through the campus near the medical library that day, must have been startled at the sight of a middle-aged man walking across campus with tears streaming down his face.

My beloved Ted might be dying. I couldn't stand it. Then came worse news.

Further tests revealed that the cancer cells in his leg had come from his lung. It was actually lung cancer that had grown slowly and symptom-free for years, and was now spreading, not just to his leg bone, but to other parts of his body as well. His situation was hopeless and he was given one year, at the most, to live. I was devastated. Ted, on the other hand, seemed to accept it with a calm resignation that enabled us to have a sensible conversation about it.

"Well," I declared, "if we only have a year, let's make it the best year possible. Let's forget everything else and go travelling. We'll do everything we've always wanted to do, see everything we have ever wanted to see, just the two of us!"

Ted agreed whole-heartedly, then two nights later, our world imploded. Ted developed a horrific headache that no pill could reach. I telephoned his oncologist, who told me to take Ted to the hospital immediately. He met us there, saw to it that Ted was admitted, put to bed and immediately sedated.

The next day, more tests were done and the news kept getting worse. Our year had been snatched away from us. The cancer cells had invaded Ted's spinal cord and were seeping into his brain. The best they could do now was keep him as pain-free as possible until the end. When would that be? Probably in only a few weeks. They would keep him in the hospital for two weeks and then send him home, or to a hospice if we so desired.

All I wanted was to be at Ted's side *now*, 24/7, to shut out the rest of the world and just focus on him, and that is exactly what I did.

For the first two nights, I slept on a cot in his

hospital room. Or tried to sleep. Every hour or so, a nurse or attendant would interrupt to check Ted. By the third day I was so sleep-deprived that I knew I couldn't continue, so I hired someone to be with Ted from 10 p.m. to 6 a.m. each night so that I could go home and get some sleep.

A nightmare is something that occurs while sleeping, but I was encountering the reverse: Each morning after I opened my eyes, I entered the living nightmare of what was happening to my partner and lover, Ted.

On his third day in the hospital, Ted lost sight in one eye. The eyelid drooped and then closed. The next day, something went haywire with his internal sense of body temperature; he felt he was burning up, and felt comfortable only with ice packs continually administered to his neck and forehead. Then he lost the ability to speak. I obtained one of those children's tablets whose writings could be erased by lifting up the plastic sheet that covered the writing surface. During the second week, he lost the ability to swallow and had to be hooked up to an intravenous drip for all his nutrition.

I decided against a hospice. I wanted to be his caregiver until the end.

He lost weight very rapidly, and on the day I took

him home, he looked terribly emaciated, but he could still walk, with my help. The nurses had trained me in the use of the intravenous drip, and had taught me how to administer the shots that kept Ted reasonably free from the otherwise unbearable pain.

There was a small bedroom adjacent to our master bedroom, with a connecting door between, that I set up for Ted. I gave him a small, tinkling, hand bell he could use to summon me when I was not with him. I confined myself to the bedrooms and the kitchen, which were close by. Although I am usually a sound sleeper, the sound of that bell would jolt me awake instantly.

A visiting nurse came by each evening to check on us and monitor Ted. One night she said to me as she left, "The end is near." Sure enough, the sound of the bell woke me in the wee hours of the morning. Ted indicated he needed to go to the bathroom, so I helped him hobble there and then back. As we approached his bed, he sagged. I was unable to hold him up. He sank to the floor and sat propped up against the side of his bed. I sat beside him and took him in my arms as he looked at me, heaved a huge sigh, and died.

How long I sat there cradling Ted, I don't know.

S. Stanley Gordon

Eventually, I was able to get to the telephone and called Michael, asking him to come and help me get Ted's body back onto the bed. By now, it was early morning. Michael was there within minutes.

The rest of that day is fuzzy, but I remember Rhoda arriving. Someone must have also called my three muses, because Gloria, Evelyn and Nancy arrived and took over. I don't know how I could have managed without them. They put me to bed. They arranged for the funeral, to be held a week hence. Using my address book, they made innumerable phone calls. They engaged a caterer for the after-funeral gathering at the house.

I was in a daze...undoubtedly in self-protective shock. At some point later that day, I got out of bed and, in my pajamas, wandered into the kitchen where my muses were busily engaged. "Give me something to do," I mumbled. "I need to have something to do or I'm going to go crazy."

They quickly devised some task—I don't remember what—to keep me occupied. Soon, two men from the mortuary arrived and carried Ted's body to a waiting vehicle. Seeing that sent me back to my bed.

The next day, I felt strong enough to get dressed. Rhoda had her family to look after, but my three ladies arrived early to make breakfast and continue the phone calls. There are no words to describe how grateful I was —and still am—for their devotion during that trying period.

During the following days, Ted's sister and her husband arrived and stayed at the house with me. One of my nephews from Philadelphia also arrived. We were particularly close, since I had helped him get through a bad patch a year previously when a girl he loved rejected him. At least the house was not empty nor was I left alone.

My words at the funeral were brief: "Ted often told me that, even though he believed in God, when he died he did not want any clergy officiating. He wanted that person to be someone who loved him dearly, and I certainly qualify for that." I added some words about how much he was loved by so many people. What I desperately wanted to say was, "Goodbye, sweet Ted...I will always miss you," but each time I rehearsed the words, I broke into tears. In the end, I left the words unsaid, except in my heart.

Other people spoke also, some in tears. Afterward, everyone went to my house. Ted had always wanted his "wake" to be a party, a celebration. I encouraged that, even though I was too physically and emotionally exhausted to do more than sit and watch.

Attendance was huge, which did not surprise me; Ted was loved by so many. Someone brought balloons. As they were released and floated skyward, there were murmurs of "Goodbye, Ted. God bless." Though I knew in my mind it was silly to think of Ted's spirit floating up with those balloons, the symbolism was too strong to resist, and I had to once again fight back tears.

Two days later, my houseguests departed and I was left alone. There was an occurrence about that time I hesitate to speak about as it may make me out to be a real "kook," but it did happen, and I'm not crazy, so here goes.

It began while Ted's sister, Marie, was still in the house. A large photo of Ted, one of my favorite pictures of him, was mounted in a frame and hung on a wall leading to our "party room" and bar. This room was at the extreme rear of the house, far from any street traffic. There was only one way to or from that room.

The day after the funeral, while all of my houseguests were in the front living room, I walked back to the bar to get something. As I passed Ted's photo, I noticed that it was hanging at a crooked angle. I assumed that someone had inadvertently brushed against it the day before, so I straightened the picture and rejoined the others. Twenty minutes later, I had to return to the bar to get something else. No one had left the living room in that interval.

Again, the picture was sharply askew. Well, I reasoned, I had done a lousy job of straightening it before. This time I made sure it was correctly and firmly in place.

It happened twice more that day. These last two times, I got goose bumps.

The next day, after my guests had gone, I made a point of passing that photo several times. It remained straight. I must confess I lost it. "Damn you, Ted!" I shouted aloud, "You did it for your sister, now do it for me!" What I didn't think about until later was that it was I who saw that picture, not Ted's sister. Maybe I was simply overwrought. Maybe traffic vibrations had reached back that far, though no other hanging pictures had moved. Maybe…but I don't think so.

I had been relatively dry-eyed up to this point, but now the dam broke. I had fiercely resolved never to cry in front of the other people; that was such a downer. But in private, my tears had a life of their own. They came unbidden, and they came in torrents.

My five dogs had dwindled to two, Humphrey and Scarlett, who were brother and sister, and they were my solace. Each time I broke down at home, they would come bounding to my side, nuzzling and licking me, as though they knew what I was going through and were comforting me.

I have read that the death of a long-time mate is the most severe adjustment a person can face, and I can attest that it is true. Half of me had been torn away, and what was left seemed less than half a person. All my joy was gone. All *feeling* was gone, and all that remained was a constant, empty hollowness.

Now I understood why so often the surviving spouse does not survive that long.

If this is how it's going to be from now on, I decided, life cannot go on. Then I thought of my kids and grandkids, and I made a conscious vow to myself: *I'll wait a year and if, at the end of that year, I still feel this way, I will find the best way to end it all.*

My Two Wives and Three Husbands

ALONE

Time is a great healer, and a year later, though I was still crying—it took three years for that to stop—all thoughts of suicide were gone. I had to face starting yet another life, one without Ted. The first step had to be to move away from the place where reminders of him shouted at me from every corner.

It took a while, but eventually I found a wonderful house on St. Ives Drive in the Hollywood Hills overlooking the famous Sunset strip. Built on the side of a hill, it had three levels, with a sweeping view of the city, clear to the ocean. Across the street, behind director George Cukor's large house, was the cottage where Katharine Hepburn nursed Spencer Tracy up to his death. My next-door neighbor was Eve Arden of "Our Miss Brooks" TV fame, who was now a sweet, elderly lady. It was arranged for Michael and his family to move into the big house in Sherman Oaks that I was vacating.

Although I loved my new home from first sight, there was one strange aspect to it that puzzled me. Years later, I saw a film starring George Clooney, entitled "A Dangerous Mind," which was based on a book written by Chuck Barris, a TV producer famous for "The Gong Show." In his book, Barris literally claimed he was secretly a CIA agent, and had performed many nefarious deeds, including assassinations. Everyone thought it was an ingenious satire, and, of course, totally untrue. I am not so sure.

My new house had belonged to that same Chuck Barris, who vacated it shortly before I bought it. The puzzling aspect I mentioned was the fact that every window was covered with heavy metal bars, and every outside door had an additional door of heavy metal, with its own ultra-secure locks. My first act, before moving in, was to remove all of that metal, and while doing so, I recall thinking, *Gee, that guy was really paranoid!*

On the lower level of the house, I discovered a small room whose view windows had been replaced with thick stained glass. The room contained a simple shower and an exposed toilet. There were two heavy floor-to-ceiling beams, and attached to each, at shoulder height, were heavy metal rings—nothing else. Very dungeon-like! *Hmmmm*, I thought. Not knowing what to do with that room, I left it "as is," and turned it into the laundry room.

Also on the lower level was a library, which was bright, with a pleasant outlook. But—as the agent had shown me before I bought the house—pushing a hidden button under one of the bookshelves caused half of that wall to swing open—revealing another room! That room was long and narrow, its walls sporting more shelves. *Well*, I told myself, *it probably was built to be a wine cellar...though why the cloak-and-dagger secret door?*

There was a row of electronic buttons along the inside wall of this "secret" room, opposite the swinging door, to which I did not give any particular thought at the time. Several days before I was to move in, however, I decided to revisit the house to confirm some measurements. It was early evening, and I arrived alone. Luckily, electricity service had been established, so I had lights.

After doing my measuring, I went downstairs to have another look at that secret room. I pushed the hidden button. The wall swung open. I went inside. *Yes*, I thought, *I think I'll store my wine here.* Then, as I started to exit, I once again noticed that row of buttons. *Hmmmm,* I thought, *what could Barris have installed all these buttons to do?*

Off-handedly, I pushed each of them, one-after-another, to see what would happen, which was silly because, naturally, whatever they were for, they would no longer be in use. After another few minutes of thinking about the room, I pushed open the swinging wall and stepped into the library, walking backward as I closed the door.

Hearing a click, I wheeled around to find myself facing two uniformed men, each holding a revolver aimed at my head! "Whoa!" I thrust my arms skyward. "I'm the new owner!" They demanded proof, and only lowered their weapons after I had thoroughly satisfied them. It frustrated me that, in spite of their numerous repeated questions, which I answered, they refused to answer any of my questions. How did they get here so fast? And the doors were all still locked, so they must have had keys, I guessed. The next morning I had the locks changed and those buttons de-activated!

At the time, I wondered if Barris had perhaps been

dealing in drugs, or was worried about kidnappers, or was simply one of those paranoid eccentrics, but after seeing his film, I wonder if his comment about working for the CIA in "A Dangerous Mind" was actually true!

Anyway, the house was lovely, the view fantastic, and I made it into a cozy nest.

For the next few years, I focused on work and friends. Despite—or maybe because of—emptiness I still felt inside, I made it a point to say "Yes" to every social invitation that came my way. Outwardly, I maintained my countenance, laughing at jokes, reacting as expected, but inside I still felt hollow.

By the fourth year, the hopeless romantic that I had always been began to re-assert itself within me, and I began to think of finding love again. But I was now sixty-seven. I had enjoyed twenty years of happiness with Ted. Was it reasonable to expect lightning to strike yet again at my advanced age? Probably not, but I was darned well going to give it another chance and find out!

The question was no longer "if," but "how." I was too old for the singles bars. It would have to be through friends and acquaintances, and, boy, did they try. Blind dates became routine, as friends "fixed me up" with one after another prospective lover. The magic, however, eluded me. Still, I forged ahead, always hoping.

At this time, I had what I consider one of my very few paranormal experiences, and it involved my dogs. For some reason, which I can't remember now, I had to go to New York for a few days, so I deposited Humphrey and Scarlett at the Sherman Oaks house where they had grown up. They would be comfortable there, and my grandkids would love it. Barbara had by now moved into the guesthouse, after her mother had died a year earlier.

Two days later, I was startled out of a deep sleep by the sound of Humphrey barking ferociously in my ear. As I awoke, I shouted, "Humphrey! Shut up!" only to realize I was alone in my quiet New York hotel room and Humphrey was thousands of miles away. Still, his barking had been so loud, so persistent, so real, *Oh, oh*, I thought, *something must have happened. I'd better call the kids.* Looking at my watch, which read exactly 8 a.m., I realized that would mean it was 5 a.m. in California— too early to call, especially if my intuition proved wrong. Besides, if something bad *had* occurred, they would call me. It was undoubtedly just a dream welling up from my overactive imagination. Just a dream. I put it out of my mind.

But the uneasy feeling didn't go away, so later that day I placed the call. Rhoda answered. After the usual greetings, I zeroed in.

"Is everyone okay?" I inquired.

"Yes," she replied. "We're all fine."

"And the dogs…. are Humphrey and Scarlett okay?" I slipped in.

"It's funny you should ask. Early this morning, Humphrey woke all of us with the loudest barking I ever heard. He wouldn't let up, and just kept barking and barking. Finally, Barbara got up to check the back yard and found that Scarlett had fallen into the pool and was swimming back and forth, trying to find the way out. Humphrey was frantically racing around the pool's edge, barking his head off. We got Scarlett out and Humphrey quieted down. I'm sure he woke up the entire neighborhood, he was so loud."

"Yes, I know," I said. "You won't believe this, but I heard him in New York…he woke me up. It was 5 a.m. there, wasn't it?"

"No, I looked at the clock as Barbara rushed out. It was exactly eight o'clock," Rhoda explained.

"Are you sure?"

"Yes, I'm sure," she assured.

233

Well, if it happened at eight o'clock California time, then I heard it three hours before it happened! Ooooo, that's spooky. Later, when I related this story to my friend, Gloria, who leans toward believing in the supernatural, she explained it as "parallel universes." I can't quite wrap my mind around that concept. I'm just too practical. And yet, how to explain it?

Actually, later on, another interesting thing occurred involving the dogs. They were both getting on in years—thirteen years to be exact. Veterinarians say that, for a standard poodle, that is equivalent to seventy-eight years in the life of a human.

One day, Humphrey lay down and would not move. He refused food or water. I sensed this was the end. So I gathered him in my arms, put him into the car and drove to the veterinarian, who confirmed it. The doctor administered a fatal shot to Humphrey, while I patted his head. He closed his eyes and died.

I cried. Anyone who has lost a beloved pet knows the feeling. And his death reminded me of Ted.

The next day, Scarlett went into a funk. She lost her appetite and her personality, and just sort of moped about all day, staying as close to me as possible. They had never been separated. I gave her as much love and attention as I could, but nothing helped. This went on, day after day.

Then she snapped out of it, regained her appetite and her personality, and was back to her former self. I looked at the calendar. It was six months, almost to the day since Humphrey had died. Do the math. For her, six months is equivalent to thirty-six months, or three years, for me. That's precisely how long it took for me to stop crying over Ted. Our mourning periods were identical. I find that fascinating.

Through Barbara's cousin, Elise, and her now lover, Aviva, I had met many lesbians. At a party one day, two of them approached me and said, "We're planning to have a baby through artificial insemination, and we have chosen you as our ideal donor. Would you do that for us?"

I did not know these women well, but felt deeply flattered. *So,* I thought, *why not?*

"Sure," I replied, "but first I have to clear this with my son and daughter-in-law."

The next day, I told Michael and Rhoda about the proposition and was startled to see both their faces blanche. "What's wrong?" I uttered. "I would have nothing to do with the child's welfare or upbringing."

Rhoda spoke first. "Knowing you, that wouldn't be

true. You couldn't help feeling and being involved."

To that, my son quickly added, "I guess it's selfish of me, but I don't want to share you."

"Then of course I won't do it," I immediately assured them.

While their reaction was unexpected, as I thought about it I was even more flattered than by the lesbians' request.

Parentage is a potent subject, and soon I found myself thinking about my parents and what their lives may have been like in Russia, ultimately prompting me to sign up for a tour to visit Russia.

All I knew about my parents' hometown was that it was a small village near Kiev, called "Shpuhla" (the closest English spelling I can come up with). When our group arrived in Kiev, I contrived, with the reluctant help of our local guide, to hire a taxi to take me to the village, which I had located on a map I procured from the hotel. It was all very cloak-and-dagger because, even though Gorbachev was then in power and had begun his reforms, foreign visitors were still not allowed to deviate from a tour's schedule.

Money talks, however, and after concocting an

elaborate cover story in case we were stopped by the authorities, a cab driver agreed to drive me to Shpuhla, while the others toured Kiev. Luckily, we never had to use that cover story.

The village turned out to be even smaller than I had imagined. One short row of stores facing a park-like square comprised downtown. I wandered into each of the stores asking, in Yiddish, "Does anyone here speak Yiddish?" As an aside: Growing up, I spoke English to my parents, and they answered me in Yiddish. It wasn't until I was an adult that I discovered I could speak Yiddish!

Blank but curious stares were my only answers. I had hoped there might be some Jewish survivors of the Nazi's march through this region, but apparently not. All had been killed—some, I later learned, with the willing cooperation of Russians.

As I sat on a bench in that village square, under a huge and very old tree, I suddenly imagined my parents sitting under that very tree. A staggering revelation swept over me: If my parents, still in their teens, had not had the guts to board a ship and cross the ocean to a land where they did not even know the language, they, too, would have been murdered...and I would not exist! What a

237

shame that I had never learned more about their background while they were still living. Kids can be so stupid in that regard. Certainly, I had been.

Well, enough reverie, now back to reality.

Back home at our office headquarters, I discovered that there were problems. Dick Mast was having trouble relinquishing control. He was micromanaging everything our sons did, inappropriately and unjustly, I thought. So I did some thinking, and sat my frustrated son down for a private talk.

Michael had often expressed a desire to raise his children in a rural environment, much like the Coos Bay/ North Bend area of Oregon where Rhoda's extended family resided. "It's clear to me," I told him, "that you kids are not going to take over the business." He nodded in agreement. "Then now," I assured him, "is the right time for you to move to Oregon, like you've always talked about."

With some financial help from me, that is exactly what Michael and his family did.

It proved a good move for them: Michael established an accounting business that thrived, and Rhoda found an outlet for her culinary creativity, becoming the "bagel queen" of the area. Their children loved having so many cousins nearby.

When my grandkids were small, I had promised that, as each graduated from high school, I would take him or her on a two-week trip to anywhere in the world they desired. No parents allowed...just the two of us. I recommend this to every grandparent...during those two weeks you will bond forever.

Grandson Charles was approaching his high school graduation. He had been awarded a five-year scholarship to the University of Oklahoma. As his summer recess approached, he reminded me about my promise. He chose England and Scotland, and I made the necessary plans and reservations. Before we met for the trip, Charles had spent a month or so doing volunteer work for his church, and, at this point, seemed to be emulating his parents in espousing fundamentalist religious views.

Even so, it was a shock when, as we met just prior to leaving for the airport, he announced, "I've decided to give up the scholarship and go to a Bible college instead. I want to become a minister." It took all of my acting skills to maintain a calm demeanor as I responded, "Well, Charles, if that's what you want, I'm behind you all the way." To myself, however, I thought, *Hmmm! I've got two weeks to work on this kid!*

A few days later, in London, I planted my seed. "You know, Charles, I've been thinking about your decision. Maybe you're making a mistake in giving up that scholarship. Maybe it would be wise for you to go to Oklahoma for a year and, if you still want to go to Bible college, make the switch then. The Bible college would still be there, but if you give up the scholarship now in order to go to Bible college, and after a year you discover it wasn't what you wanted after all, the scholarship will no longer be there for you."

He made no comment, so I could only hope that he would think about it. A few days later, we had lunch with a lady I knew in London, and she innocently asked Charles what his plans were now that he had finished high school. I had not told her anything about that subject, so I was elated when, after hearing his plan to dump the scholarship in favor of the Bible college, she repeated, almost word for word, the suggestion I had made. I kept my mouth shut for a change, and hoped he wouldn't think I had primed her.

Fade out, fade in, he took the scholarship, went on five years later to receive another scholarship for two and a half years more at the University of Washington in Seattle, and is now a computer guru with a high-level position in "silicone valley." Oh, yes, and he is also an atheist, though not by my doing, I swear!

Back in Los Angeles, my search for love went on. And on. And on.

Evelyn introduced me to a male dancer friend of hers who was extremely attractive, and we began dating. For a time it looked promising, but after a few months I realized it wasn't the real thing and broke it off.

It happened again with a professional man I met. We were attracted to each other physically. He was a great kisser (good kissing is really an art) and a very imaginative bedmate—two formidable attributes, you must agree. But, alas, after encountering some bizarre behavior on his part, I discovered that he was a drug addict. Pity! I wanted no part of that scene, so I ended the relationship.

Well, I thought, I have to accept the fact that my love life is over. Nine years had passed since Ted died. I was now seventy-two years old. Seventy-two! Who was I kidding? Sure, I looked ten years younger, but still...*get real*, I told myself. *Forget it, it ain't gonna happen!*

Some friends knew a couple that had recently found

each other through the *Los Angeles Times*. This was before today's computer-dating avenues became so popular. The *Times*, in their "Dateline" section, ran columns twice a week titled "Men Seeking Women," "Women Seeking Men," "Men Seeking Men" and "Women Seeking Women." How the world had changed! My buddies persuaded me to place an ad. "Okay," I uttered in resignation, "but this is my last gasp. After this I'm giving up the search."

We conferred at length on what the ad should say. My inclination was to use the word "attractive," but they convinced me that "handsome" would get more bites. In the end the ad read, "Handsome silver fox seeks mature man for meaningful relationship. Theatre, tennis, travel." Then followed the Times phone number, and a special box number that gave the caller a verbal message I had recorded. If the caller liked my message, he would leave a message of his own and his phone number for me to call him back.

My recorded message, besides giving the general area where I lived, mentioned my twenty-year love and his death from cancer. I added that I was hoping lightning might strike again, and closed with, "Is that thunder I hear in the distance?" How corny could I get?

Despite the drama-queen ending, I got a fair number of responses. It is remarkable how much can be gleaned from a telephone call. Some were obvious flakes, some were silly "queens;" I ignored those. One gave me a number that was no longer in service. Two sounded possible, and another one sounded very promising. I met each of the "possibles" for lunch. They were nice people, but no bells rang. I then proceeded to dial the number whose voice and message had especially intrigued me. His name, he had stated, was Joe Henry. When a woman answered, I hung up.

Wait! Perhaps, I reasoned, *I had transposed some numbers when I wrote down the phone number I heard on his message.*

I tried every possible combination of those numbers, but none were correct. *Maybe I had simply misdialed the original number.* I dialed it again. This time a man answered.

My Two Wives and Three Husbands

JOE

"Hello."

"Is this Joe Henry?"

"Speaking."

"This is Stanley Gordon. I called earlier and a woman answered."

"Oh," he said, "that was my wife."

I was speechless. Sensing my confusion, he added, "We're in the process of separating, and I am getting ready to move into my own condo."

Ah, this I could understand. "I know what you're going through...I've been there myself." Because he was busy with his impending move, he could not meet with me for several days, so we made a date for dinner at the Tam O'Shanter Inn, a restaurant we both knew, a week hence. I liked his voice. It resonated with stability and maturity. But then he told me he was six-feet-eight-inches tall. I had images of a hulking football-player physique, or a skinny, string-bean type. Hmmmm.

He turned out to be neither. I sat in a chair facing the restaurant's reservation desk and caught a view of his back as he walked past me to approach the desk. He was well-proportioned and I was struck by his posture. Most tall men tend to slouch in a misguided attempt to appear shorter, but this man held his head and shoulders high. I liked that. I said to myself, he is self-confident, secure in who he is. Then he turned around.

We looked at each other...and the bells began to peal. Joe told me later that his heart leaped! We were shown to a table, ordered dinner and began to talk. Two hours later, we were still talking. My heart told me he was someone special, and I had a fast decision to make. Joe told me that he was fifty-nine years old. Normally I do not mention my age, especially not on the first date, but this was serious! If the thirteen-year difference in our ages was going to be a stumbling block, I wanted to know it then and now, not later when it could hurt us both. So I told him my age and held my breath. The news didn't elicit any visible reaction, so I took that as a conditional acceptance, though my inner voice warned, *when he thinks it over, he'll probably reject me.* To avoid any pressure, I suggested that he call me soon to arrange another date.

I heaved a sigh of relief when he called the very next morning.

Just after his call, I received a call from my friend, Nancy Freed, whose actor husband, Bert, had died some years earlier. Before she could tell me the purpose of her call, I bubbled, "Nancy! Last night I met the man I'm going to marry!"

"Ooooo," she enthused. "Tell me about him."

"His name is Joe, he's six-feet-eight-inches tall, and...." That's as far as I got before she exclaimed, "You're talking about Joe Henry! And what happened to his *wife*?"

After I picked myself up off of the floor, I managed to utter, "How in the world do you know Joe Henry?" It turned out that Nancy, a public relations professional, had done PR work some years earlier for the Art Center College of Design in Pasadena, where Joe was senior vice president. She had gotten to know Joe and his wife, Wanda Gae, quite well and was fond of both of them. Small world!

For our second date, I cooked dinner at my house for just the two of us. Joe brought me flowers. Flowers!! Now, I am not the world's best chef, but that meal was perfect. Or maybe anything would have tasted wonderful that night. We were both on cloud nine, and we knew this was *it*.

Without making any verbal commitments, we began seeing each other exclusively. Joe had retired at an early age from the Art Center and was extremely active volunteering at several nonprofit organizations in the Pasadena area. His condo was in Monrovia, beyond Pasadena, a rather long distance from my Hollywood Hills home, but love conquers all, and we saw each other every weekend, as well as once or twice during the week.

When we told each other what we each were feeling, it was no surprise to either of us. We finally agreed that, as much as we were both anxious to live together, we would hold off for a year. Just to make sure. With age comes wisdom…and a touch of wariness.

Joe, I learned, is a PK…a "preacher's kid." His father was a United Methodist minister in Ohio, where Joe was born and spent his early years, the family having moved to Southern California when Joe was thirteen. He was twenty when, a junior at Pomona College, his mother died, and two years later his father remarried. Joe's stepmother was named Harriette; she and Joe had a good relationship. By the time I met Joe, his father had been dead for a number of years.

Joe knew from an early age that he was "different," but as I had found in my own early life, there was no ready explanation in those days for that difference. He had no interest in sports, which, with his exceptional height, was hard to justify to eager basketball coaches. He was artistic, always drawing clothes, houses and automobiles.

As a child he had a fashion doll for which a seamstress aunt turned his designs into garments. A large dollhouse was in a constant state of redecoration. When he became a student at Pomona College, he majored in fine art. Even so, there was nothing effeminate about Joe. He exuded strength and stability and maturity. When I met him, his graying hair was accompanied by a grayer mustache on a patrician and distinguished face.

Throughout his youth, Joe had managed to successfully suppress any overt homosexual inclinations. His father, who had adored his maternal grandfather, wanted a similar relationship with his own grandchild, and told Joe (the only child) in no uncertain terms that Joe was being relied on to provide that grandchild. Joe, in turn, was determined to live up to his father's expectations.

Joe dated girls, much as I had done in my college years. Unlike me, however, Joe remained celibate. He had decided on a career as a fashion designer, but after winning a California statewide collegiate design competition during his junior year in college, he recognized that pursuing that plan would place him in a gay environment he must, at all costs, avoid if he was to fulfill his father's wish. So he abandoned fashion design and, once out of college, decided to pursue the business end of fashion as a management trainee with a local department store. It seemed a safer environment in which to hide, but still be a part of the fashion "scene." After only two years, a candidate for a full buyer's position, he decided that management wasn't how he wanted to spend his life.

Serendipity, again: A career counseling session with Pomona's Dean of Men, and personal uncertainty about the direction he wanted to take, led him to accept an open position in the college's alumni office.

For the remainder of his professional life, Joe was a college administrator, first at Pomona College and subsequently at the California Institute of Technology (Caltech) and, finally, at the Art Center College of Design. At the Art Center, he moved into the position of Senior Vice President and Assistant Director of the college. He ended 21 years with the Art Center as Founding Director of a new branch campus in Switzerland, returning to California to retire after his final five years.

In his twenties, Joe had been engaged twice, but ultimately broke both engagements.

His most meaningful early relationship started while he was still a student. And it was with a man...a chaste "buddy" friendship with a young man named Ken. Joe and Ken were good friends for eight years, with nothing overtly gay on the surface, though each sensed that the other was gay. That is, until one night, Ken made "the move"...actually, an overture that sent Joe hurtling into the night in panic. They broke off all communication.

Eleven months later Joe, still a virgin in every sense, married Wanda Gae. He felt it was a genuine love match, replete with closeness and excellent rapport, though the sexuality issue was a hurdle he would have to climb over.

It would be thirty years before Ken and Joe renewed their friendship, just before I entered Joe's life. Ken now lives in the Palm Springs area with his long-time partner. Joe and I enjoy visiting them whenever we go to the desert.

Interestingly, after Joe and Wanda Gae fulfilled Joe's father's dream, presenting him with a grandson, grandfather and grandson never developed that dreamed-of close relationship. Pity, once again!

Joe's contract with the Art Center allowed him to retire with significant benefits when his five-year stint in Switzerland ended. All that time, he continued suppressing his homosexual yearnings, but now, facing an early retirement at age fifty-five, no longer having a career to focus on, his struggle with his own sexuality became more and more difficult. After several years of soul-searching and counseling, both psychiatric and religious, Joe "came out" to his wife.

I am in awe of the fact that Joe managed to suppress his homosexuality for over forty years. There were moments when he almost succumbed. Once, he made a short trip to Paris from Switzerland, with the express intention of having a gay experience...but couldn't bring himself to go through with it. Again later, in Los Angeles, he made some brief forays to a local gay cinema, but could not make the overtures necessary to connect with another man. That's what I call incredible will power and integrity. And Joe is honorable, through and through. I often describe him as the "finest man I have ever known." How lucky I am!

Joe's separation from Wanda Gae was entirely amicable. After 30 years of marriage, including raising a son (also named Michael, and also an accountant!), Wanda Gae accepted Joe's homosexuality and was very supportive. She is a truly remarkable person. They remained living together, even while Joe went through two six-month-affairs with men he met through the *L.A. Times*. Joe was ready to move into his own condo when he answered my ad…and the rest is history!

During my first meeting with Wanda Gae, which occurred at a theatre, she approached me with outstretched hand and said, "You must be Stanley." To which this wiseacre replied, "Dr. Livingstone, I presume?"

She laughed at my lame joke and we became good friends. In fact, I later remarked to Joe, "If I were straight I would have married Wanda Gae, not you." A straightforward, no-nonsense lady, Wanda Gae combines an intellectual bent with a compassionate nature. She and I think alike; we really are kindred spirits. How fortunate!

Of course, more fortunate was the immediate closeness that attracted Joe to me, and me to him. Everyone has idiosyncrasies, frequently labeled "faults" or "virtues," depending upon viewpoint. The alchemy that love creates is the ability to embrace the virtues and laugh at the faults as mere foibles. Joe and I laugh a lot!

One example: Joe has a tendency to ramble on, complaining about small annoyances. One day, he was doing just that. I tried to be the sympathetic listener, all the time smiling inwardly at the trivial nature of his complaint. My attempt at keeping a straight face, however, must have been unsuccessful, because he suddenly stopped in mid-sentence, looked at me, and heaving a big sigh, said in all seriousness, "Well, you know…it isn't easy being me!" I fell on the floor laughing; he quickly joined me.

As the end of our first year of dating approached, Joe and I began talking in earnest about living together. But where? We both loved my home in the Hollywood hills, but that would have meant frequent long commutes for

Joe, who had become a "pillar of society" in the Pasadena area: President of the Pasadena Senior Center and Wellness Community-Foothills boards, board member of Methodist Hospital, volunteer fundraiser for his *alma mater*, Pomona College, and a board or committee member of several other local charities. Joe was widely known and highly respected.

I, on the other hand, assiduously avoided serving any community organization. I gave money instead of time, so it would be no hardship for me to live in Pasadena. Joe's small, cozy condo would not be suitable, so we began house hunting in Pasadena.

A real estate agent-friend of Joe's told us that she had found the perfect house for us, and when we went to see it, we immediately agreed. No need to see any others, it happened to be adjacent to the Art Center campus in the Linda Vista hills, just above the Rose Bowl.

I sold my home in the Hollywood Hills and we made the move. My remaining poodle, Scarlett, had long since died, so we were a dogless couple.

While moving into our new home in Pasadena, Joe and I made a conscious decision that we were going to be an "out" gay couple in the community. Instead of appearing with Wanda Gae at all the social functions occasioned by his various organizations, he would appear with me. We would make no bones about it...no pretenses. Pasadena was a conservative community, founded by "old money" families, and I had some trepidation. How would I be accepted? Would Joe be ostracized?

We needn't have feared. With rare exception, I was embraced wholeheartedly, and our gay-couple status was not only accepted, but also warmly received. It helped, I'm sure, that Joe was not only widely known and respected, but also beloved by all who knew him. And Wanda Gae's support for both of us also played a big role.

One of Joe's traits that I liked to laugh about was his desire to have everything done "his way." In fact, he worried that his compulsive tendency might clash with my own highly self-sufficient background. Little did he know that, at this stage of my life, I longed to be relieved of making the myriad small decisions that constitute day-to-day living. It was a win-win situation for me to say, "You like that task done a certain way? Fine! Be my guest!" and Joe was delighted to take over the function.

The only problem this caused was, as a result, Joe did or supervised almost everything, and I felt a little—

just a little, mind you—guilty. Joe saw to it that our lovely home was always spotless. He did the laundry and the ironing. He worked in the garden. He kept my clothes in pristine condition. He did all the packing and the unpacking before, during and after our travels. Some would say I had it made!

Nonetheless, now and then my guilt would rise to the surface as Joe perspired, packing our suitcases. And I would volunteer with, "How can I help you?" Joe's invariable answer, as I knew it would be, was, "You can help me most by simply staying out of my way!" to which my stock reply is, "That's one of the things I do best."

I did propose, however, that I take over the cooking —I, whose culinary skills were severely limited—and discovered there was actually a pretty decent cook hiding inside of me, just waiting to be let loose. The bottom line is that, with practice, I got rather good.

As a house-warming gift, Wanda Gae went to the trouble of writing down, in longhand, the recipes for many of Joe's favorite dishes. Now that's a classy lady! That little book has proven a Godsend to this neophyte chef.

The Methodist Hospital in Arcadia held an annual

dinner for its board members and spouses, which was also attended by a group of United Methodist women from California and the Pacific islands. Many came from conservative rural areas. It was the custom, at these dinners, for the hospital president to introduce each board member, who stood to the applause, and then introduce the member's spouse, who also stood to the applause. Joe was a board member, and I was sitting beside him my first time attending one of those dinners. *Ho ho*, I thought, *this will be interesting!*

When Joe's name was called, he stood and everyone applauded. I waited with bated breath. I would be introduced next...but with what designation? The hospital president didn't miss a beat as he said, "And Joe Henry's partner, Stanley Gordon." I stood up and everyone applauded. I sat down. That, I knew, was a "first" for the Methodist Hospital. Over subsequent years, the terms "husband" or "wife" or "spouse" were dropped for "partner," and that is how it remained.

The Pasadena Rotary Club, of which Joe is a longtime member, publishes a roster each year, which contains the photo of each member, along with address and professional particulars about the member, followed by the name of the member's spouse. For the first time ever, in 1997, the roster listed Stanley Gordon as Joe Henry's spouse. Now other same-sex partners are listed also. Progress!

And so it went. We were treated as a married couple, just like any other couple, and we reveled in it. The times were changing, and we felt we had an active part in that evolution, at least in the Pasadena area.

Joe and I have carried our openness over to our frequent travels—how could we avoid it really, with Joe saying, "Darling, would you please pass the salt?" We have found that most travelers are eager to learn more about our relationship and others like it.

A male couple we know always traveled as "friends who live on the same block." When they expressed a desire to accompany us on a trip, we stated, "If you come with us, you have to be an 'out' gay couple, because that's how we do it." They gulped, but agreed. They did it, and told us afterward that it was the most enjoyable vacation they had ever experienced. Of course! They were free to be themselves, to relax without worrying about appearances. We encouraged them to carry that behavior into their everyday lives. Leading a double life, as most gay people have been forced to do, is a huge burden.

Having that yoke lifted is truly liberating.

Feeling his new freedom, Joe surprised even me one Halloween. We were invited to a costume party at the home of a gay friend. To my astonishment, Joe announced that he wanted to go in a serious "drag" outfit. "But, Joe!" I sputtered, "in high heels you'll be a *giant* woman!" Joe listened but was not dissuaded.

Shopping on Hollywood Blvd., where one can buy *anything*, Joe found a very becoming short-bobbed, blonde wig, four-inch high heels (size sixteen!), a brassiere (with appropriate stuffing), and pantyhose. The clerks who waited on him remained completely blasé, as though they encountered shoppers like Joe every day... and maybe they did!

The gowns on the boulevard were too expensive, so Joe went shopping at a local discount store. I wish I had gone with him because he recounted that, as he was paying for it at the checkout, the female cashier asked, "Have you tried on the dress to make sure it fits?" The world *was* advancing and faster than I had thought!

Well, Joe picked a very smart (could it be otherwise, with his fashion sense?), long evening gown. Two days before the party, Joe held a "dress rehearsal" for me, transforming himself into a very elegant—and tall—lady. The first step was to shave off his mustache, which never returned. I laughed when he had trouble balancing on those high heels, but I was also amazed by how gorgeous his long legs looked in heels. Now I understood why women endure whatever it takes to get used to them... they work a kind of visual magic for the calves.

"Joe!" I finally proclaimed, "you can't hide those fantastic gams under a long evening gown. You need a short cocktail dress!" So, back he went to the discount store and, this time, bought a stunning knee-length dress. Different clerk, same matter-of-fact attitude, and in Pasadena, no less!

On the night of the party, I donned the semi-outfit of Joe-sephine's gangster boyfriend, and off we went.

At the party, gays and straights mingled together, and I was nonplussed when one of the straight gentlemen asked Joe-sephine if "she" would accompany him to the opera one night! I lost no time in loudly proclaiming "If you take *him* you also take me!" The surprised gentleman paused—appearing to actually consider it for a moment —then, smiling, withdrew.

I suppose Joe got that long-repressed gambit out of his system that night because he has never expressed any desire to repeat it. But wow, for that one evening, he really *was* a beautiful, elegant, *extremely tall woman!*

Early in our relationship, Joe and I traveled to Philadelphia, so I could introduce him to my relatives there. Now that I had "come out" to my siblings, we could all feel at ease, confident that their children knew the score about us. It turned out our confidence was fully justified, with everyone treating Joe as one of the family. What a contrast to the way I used to feel when returning to Philadelphia for a visit before I "came out!" Back then, I was tense, always acting a role that felt foreign, fidgeting anxiously for the time to pass quickly. This visit was a pleasure: I felt relaxed, and really got to enjoy my relatives.

When we moved into our house in Pasadena, Joe was serving as President of the Pasadena Senior Center board. One day, he received a call from a staff member at the center, asking us to attend a class being held that evening that was part of a series on how to adjust to retirement. ABC-TV News would be there, the staff member explained, and she wanted to insure a full house for the cameras. So we went.

There was, indeed, a cameraman there, as well as a

young producer from ABC. During a break in the filming, Joe, as president of the board, was introduced to the producer, and they engaged in conversation. When Joe returned to his seat beside me, he reported, "The producer asked if my wife was here tonight, and I told him I am gay, living with a man who is here with me." We both smiled. Nothing further was said about the subject.

A few days later, I was sitting at my desk at home when I heard the phone ring. Joe answered it in an adjacent room; I could not hear his conversation, but suddenly he burst into my room, with a bemused expression on his face.

"That TV producer is on the phone, wanting to know if he can bring his cameraman to our house one day this week. He wants to interview us, and include us as part of his follow-up coverage of the class."

I gulped. "Well, I guess we're ready for prime time. Let her rip!"

Several days later they appeared, spending almost two hours getting footage of the two of us going about our usual household activities. Then they interviewed each of us separately, filming when we answered the producer's various off-camera questions. They left, promising to call us in advance when the segment was scheduled to be aired.

The call came a few weeks later, saying it would be aired on the "ABC Afternoon News" at 4 p.m. the following day. Of course, we set our VCR to tape it while we watched. Laura Diaz, one of the anchorwomen, introduced the Senior Center class as part of an ongoing series on "Better Living." The first few minutes showed Helen Dennis, the retirement specialist, teaching the class, followed by a few comments from class members. One of the latter was Joe, who, in answer to a question from Helen, said, "Friend relations are an important part in the transition."

Then Laura Diaz appeared again, saying, "And this is a couple that has learned a valuable lesson," at which point, there Joe and I were in living Technicolor, on our patio, as I handed Joe a glass of water and took a seat beside him. Laura Diaz's voice-over was saying, "Retired now for seven years, Joe Henry lives with his partner, Stanley Gordon."

The next shot was a close-up of Joe in our living room saying, "Retirement is a huge transition. There are a lot of people who are afraid of it." Then the camera showed a close-up of me saying, "The trick is to live with someone you love so much and enjoy so much that being together more is better than being together less. That's the trick." Then the show moved on to another topic.

As I watched myself saying those words, I said to Joe, "Ouch! How smug!" What a slap-in-the-face my words must be to those housewives who hate having their newly-retired husbands under foot all the time. Still, my words were true. Can I help it if the truth hurts?

The broadcast had not been over more than two minutes when our phone rang. It was an excited male viewer from San Marino, who breathlessly exclaimed, "I got your number from the phone book…I'm gay and I can't *believe* that ABC aired that! They treated you as just another couple. It was terrific!"

I agreed, but at four in the afternoon who other than this person would really be watching? Though the show was not repeated on the evening news hour, quite a few people, it turned out, did see it. Our next-door neighbors as well as two lesbian acquaintances called to say they had seen it. Hopefully our statement made a small dent in watchers' attitudes. Every little bit helps. Loud activists may command the news, but it is the everyday gay people living openly who bring about real change and acceptance.

Speaking of change and acceptance, I heard rumblings that Chuck, the managing optician at one of my nephew Eric's offices, was having marital problems. Chuck's wife works as a receptionist at that same office. So I was not too surprised when Chuck asked to speak with me privately. I had been acting as "Father Confessor" to more and more employees over the years, and I suppose he knew I would be sympathetic to whatever problems he needed to unload.

But Zowie! I was not prepared for this particular problem. He had, he said, all his life felt like a woman trapped in a man's body. Yes, he had fought it, gotten married, sired children, but now the feeling had grown so strong that he felt he could not go on living as a man. He had confessed all to his wife and she, to her credit, was not opposing him.

So, he asked me, "Would you present my situation to Eric and ask if I can keep working here, as a woman?" Chuck wanted to start dressing as a woman, full time, with the ultimate goal of having a sex-change operation.

Now it was confab time for Dick, Eric and myself. I especially girded myself for a huge explosion from my longtime colleague, the gruff, conservative Dick Mast. To my astonishment, he was completely supportive. "That takes real guts!" he exclaimed.

Now the question was: would patients be turned off by what may be a too-apparent man in women's clothing? We decided to perform a test. We arranged for Chuck—as Rebecca, his newly adopted female name—dressed as a woman, to meet us at an upscale restaurant for lunch.

Dick, Eric and I gathered early at a table, facing the entrance of the restaurant, anxiously awaiting Rebeca's arrival.

When she appeared, she paused momentarily, as though to let us peruse her thoroughly at a slight distance, then proceeded to our table. To us, she appeared to have broader shoulders and bigger feet than would be expected of a woman, but no one else seemed to notice. Her hair, long for a man, was styled in a woman's short bob. Rebecca seemed very much at ease, and the rest of us tried to act nonchalant. Lunch and conversation ensued a bit awkwardly, I thought, but without incident.

I paid the check, and we all departed together for the parking lot, where we said goodbye to Rebecca. I then turned to the others and said, as we rolled our eyes and shook our heads, "Wait for me here. I forgot something at the table." Going back inside, I found the waitress who had served us.

"Excuse me. Did you notice anything unusual about any of the people at our table?"

She thought for a moment, and said "No. Was someone ill?" I assured her that was not the case, and then rejoined Dick and Eric. "Well," I reported, "our waitress didn't notice anything unusual, so maybe our perception is influenced by our knowing the female Rebecca was really the male Chuck."

And that proved to be the case. We came to learn about the extensive steps that a would-be transsexual must go through: cosmetic tips, grooming, taking hormones and growing breasts. One thing the hormones cannot do is change the voice. So Rebecca had to learn to raise her voice half an octave, and to speak softly. She regularly attended preparatory classes with other pre-operative transsexuals. Most enlightening! I had no idea there were so many!

I must confess I had always looked at the transsexual issue as a strange and rare phenomenon. But now, coming face to face with someone I knew and respected going through the process, and learning more about it, I wondered if this might have been how heterosexuals felt about gays. So I learned first-hand that prejudice and fear can be shattered with knowledge and personal contact. After all, as I told that English dowager, it is an accident of birth.

While patients seemed to accept Rebecca as a woman, we worried about how her fellow-employees would react. Chuck's first step, therefore, was to send to his co-workers a long letter—too long to quote here, but here are some salient excerpts:

....for the first forty years of my life, I felt that there existed a severe incongruity between my perceived gender and my real gender. I over-compensated with two marriages and fatherhood, only to end up feeling like a liar and a cheat. I saw many therapists but they were not able to help me, and it was an issue I was afraid to face. Therefore, when I desperately returned to therapy to face myself honestly for the first time in my life, I sought out a professional who specialized in gender issues...I can tell you now that I have been on hormone therapy for about a year, and I have never felt so well in all my life...I will soon begin to live my life and work as Rebecca.

Although this will be a novel situation for us, I am confident that you can approach this adventure with the good humor and grace that I value in you all; it would be an incredible treat to have your support and understanding.

It did prove to be a problem at first. Not with the men, surprisingly, but the female employees were apprehensive. However, the sweet, likable Chuck, now the even sweeter, more charming Rebecca, soon won everybody over. His (her?) wife's acceptance, I believe, helped a great deal. To this day, they both work in the same office.

Chuck had his operation—yes, the genitals really can be changed—and, as Rebecca, she is happier than she ever was before as Chuck.

As I write these words, Joe and I have just returned from another trip to a far-away land. We determined early on that we would travel extensively as long as we had the time, the money, and the health to do so—something Ted and I missed the opportunity to do. In the sixteen years we have now been together, we have taken over thirty cruises and at least as many land trips.

Such travel has only been possible because we are both retired. Joe was fortunate to achieve an early retirement from the Art Center after his stint in Switzerland. I had a harder time extricating myself from my professional duties, until it dawned on me that my quasi-nephew, Eric, was uniquely qualified to take over from Dick and me. Eric was amenable and—after some arm-twisting on Dick—we made suitable arrangements. Hooray!

Although Joe and I are both in good health, one never knows what tomorrow will bring.

In fact, Joe has had several close calls with death. We both still laugh when we recall my outburst as he was being resuscitated from a near-fatal heart incident: "Joe, if you die on me, I'll kill you!" It's funny now because I was serious then. Two dead husbands is tragic enough... three is unacceptable. He now has an implanted pacemaker and defibrillator, and I had a heart valve replaced—with a pig valve, no less, so I am no longer entirely kosher. We appreciate each day in a way that younger couples rarely think about.

My Two Wives and Three Husbands

HAPPILY EVER AFTER

Looking back at the promiscuity of my "single life," I wonder at my total lack of moral questioning. It never occurred to me to wonder if it was "right" or "wrong." A new, enticing world opened up and I simply plunged in. The itch, and later need, was so strong, I simply scratched it.

But when it came to commitment, that was an entirely different story. I felt a strong moral obligation to be faithful, and I never violated that principal. Religion didn't enter into it...the conviction was so deep it *was* me.

Religion and I were strangers, if not enemies. Knowing how homosexuality was frowned upon by most church bodies, I avoided contact with religion...even organ music repelled me. So I was surprised when, upon learning that Joe's ex-wife, Wanda Gae, planned to lead a

36-week Bible study group at their Methodist church, I joined up. Well, I reasoned, the Bible is important, if only because everyone else seemed to know so much about it and I knew so little.

That experience was an eye-opener, for me and for the others in the class. They, being regular church-goers, took much of the Bible for granted, without too much thought. I, however, saw everything with fresh eyes, which stimulated lively discussions about not only its content but also life in general, and interpersonal relationships in particular. What resulted was a genuine bonding among the group. I did not become a "believer," but I now consider myself a questioning agnostic rather than an atheist.

The biggest benefit from the class was the eradication of my fears about religion. Quite often now, I join Joe and Wanda Gae at their church for Sunday morning service and interact warmly with other parishioners. Even though I am not a member, I have volunteered—and been welcomed—to join Joe and Wanda Gae working on a church committee to improve the congregation's outreach to the gay and lesbian community. Hopefully, in the not-too-distant future, the

Methodist denomination will cease discriminating against this one last group that has yet to be embraced fully.

When California passed its "Civil Union" law, Joe and I had signed up as domestic partners, which gave us some—though not yet all—of the rights permitted any married couple. For us, it was simply a normal progression in our own relationship together. Then, suddenly it seemed, "gay marriage" became an ideological, and quickly thereafter, political issue all over the world. It became legal in Canada, Spain, The Netherlands. In the U.S., Massachusetts was the first state to legalize "gay marriage." Personally, I never dreamed it would happen within my lifetime!

In May, 2008, the California Supreme Court ruled the state's ban on gay marriage unconstitutional, and the following month, marriage licenses began being issued to gay couples. Joe and I were ecstatic. Even though we felt, at the time, satisfied with a domestic partnership, at least we now had a choice.

Joe and I began attending weddings of gay friends. Couples we knew who had lived together for 50 years or more decided to tie the knot. Elise and Aviva, whom I had introduced to each other so long ago, got married. Joe and I attended their rites, which were performed by a lesbian rabbi, whose ceremony was so beautiful and so moving that Joe and I decided on the spot that *we* had to get married—and by that rabbi!

And we did! So, are we glad we did it? Do we feel different? Let me share a letter I sent to the *Los Angeles Times*—which they never printed, the Philistines, though we do have them to thank for our having met:

Marriage…who needs it? That's what I, and many of my gay friends, always said. My partner, Joe, and I had our lawyers arrange our financial affairs to our specifications. As an out gay couple, we had been in a faithful, committed relationship for many years. Marriage wouldn't change that. So who needed it?

But when the California Supreme Court gave us the right to marry, Joe and I decided to do it, if for no other reason than to make a statement; it wouldn't really change *us*, we thought.

Our first surprise was the enthusiasm that straight friends and acquaintances (even strangers) demonstrated upon hearing of our plans. Their expressions of joy and delight were heartwarming. And so, with the blessings and support of our closest friends, we, too, were married.

Now, weeks later, I look at myself in the mirror and ask, 'So? Do you feel any different?' After thinking about it, the answer surprises me, and asking Joe the same question, he echoes my feeling. Yes, I do feel different. I hold my head higher. I walk taller. I feel as one with my peers. The state's official seal of approval has given me legitimacy, validation... respect. I never realized they had been missing, or how important they were.

So, to people—gay and straight—who scoff at marriage, I say: Do not underestimate it. It is a rich blessing that adds stature to life. Everybody who is lucky enough to have a loving mate should do it.

Our wedding was held at our home, with forty close friends and relatives in attendance.

As a Methodist, Joe's minister was not permitted to

officiate at a gay marriage, but he was allowed to "participate" and he volunteered to read a poem during the ceremony. He chose Elizabeth Barrett Browning's sonnet, "How Do I Love Thee? Let Me Count the Ways," and by the time he was finished with his heartfelt reading there wasn't a dry eye in the house.

Joe's son, Michael, attended, as well as Joe's ex-wife, Wanda Gae, and her husband. My son could not attend— he was scheduled to give a tax seminar that weekend, so daughter-in-law Rhoda didn't come either. My fundamentalist missionary granddaughter, Danielle, had given birth to my first great-grandson a short time before, so she couldn't come. But my other three grandchildren— Charles (with wife Ana), Ilana and Talia—all flew down from Oregon and Northern California for the occasion.

Joe and I accepted the missing family members' excuses. They were completely understandable. Still, we were disappointed when the wedding came and went with no congratulations from them.

Then, the following morning, Rhoda telephoned. "*Beau-Pere*," she said (that is her favorite name for me: French for "father-in-law"), "we've always been honest with each other."

"Yes," I replied, "we always have."

"Well, I wanted to make sure that you and Joe knew that we love you very much." I was so glad that, despite her religious reservations, she called, and reassured her of our love for them.

Shortly after, an e-mail message arrived from Danielle, wishing us the best, but it was her salutation, "Dear Grandpas," that brought tears to my eyes.

Months later, she and her husband (also a fundamentalist missionary) were visiting his father (a conservative Episcopalian minister), who lives nearby in South Pasadena. When they came to see us, my grandson-in-law, with baby Alex in his arms, walked up to Joe and said to his son, "Alex, say hi to your great-grandpa Joe."

Goose bump time again!

Several people have asked me if, being married to a man, my emotional state differed from being married to a woman. I've tried to honestly re-live my feelings, the similarities and differences, and what I keep coming up with is that, while I loved my wives in the sense of caring for and about them, I was never truly *in love* with them. What I felt for my two wives was affection and responsibility. What I felt for my three husbands was romantic, gleeful, giddy. It was being hopelessly in love. There is no feeling like it, and lucky are the people who get to experience it.

What about having children? I feel blessed to have a child, and now I fully appreciate some couples' desire to adopt when they cannot procreate.

I can understand why pundits often say one has to work at marriage. I guess that's true for some, but not me and not, I hope, for many others. Sure, Emmett, my first husband, effectively killed our love, and if he had lived and welcomed me back into his life, I would have had to work at re-kindling my feelings—which, in the end, may or may not have succeeded.

However, with Ted, and now Joe, no "work" was ever necessary. Ted's last kiss made my knees just as weak as his first. Joe and I, after sixteen years, are just as much in love now as ever. Are we simply lucky? Or do too many people, in their initial search, compromise and settle for safety and security, instead of waiting for lightening to strike? I don't know the answer. I only know that, in the end, my waiting paid off.

My own ode to love is perfectly expressed in one of my favorite popular songs, written for the Broadway show, "Do Re Mi," by songwriter Jule Styne, with lyrics by Betty Comden and Adolph Green. The song is titled "Make Someone Happy," and the last stanza says it all:

Fame, if you win it,
Comes and goes in a minute.
Where's the real stuff in life to cling to?
Love is the answer.
Someone to love is the answer.
Once you've found him [or her],
Build your world around him [or her].
Make someone happy.
Make just one someone happy,
And you will be happy, too.

What makes this song even more special, in my mind, is that it's been said in countless different ways over the centuries, but it still applies to all, male or female, gay or straight, alone or coupled.

So here's to LOVE! And may you be happy, too.

My Two Wives and Three Husbands

About the Author

With this book, S. Stanley Gordon begins his fifth career. As a Doctor of Optometry, he was in private practice until his second career as a principal in a nationwide optical enterprise. Upon the sale of this business, he fulfilled a lifelong ambition to be in show business, starting at the top as a theatrical producer in New York and London. This was followed by semi-retirement as a professional consultant, and later with full retirement...or so he thought! He currently lives in Pasadena, California, with his husband, Joe Henry. His son and daughter-in-law have blessed him with four grandchildren and two great-grandchildren, with more in the offing.

My Two Wives and Three Husbands

Acknowledgement

This book would not have been possible without the emotional support and loving encouragement of my husband, Joe Henry, who has given me 16 years (and counting) of serene happiness. His ex-wife, Wanda Gae, has been of immense value as a good friend. Last but not least, I thank my lucky stars for having a publisher/editor with the humanity and wisdom of Daniel Janik…a new author's dream come true.

If you enjoyed *My Two Wives and Three Husbands* consider these other fine Books from Savant Books and Publications:

A Whale's Tale by Daniel S. Janik
Tropic of California by R. Page Kaufman
The Village Curtain by Tony Tame
Dare to Love in Oz by William Maltese
The Interzone by Tatsuyuki Kobayashi
Today I am a Man by Larry Rodness
The Bahrain Conspiracy by Bentley Gates
Called Home by Gloria Schumann
Kanaka Blues by Mike Farris
First Breath edited by Z. M. Oliver
Poor Rich by Jean Blasiar
The Jumper Chronicles by W. C. Peever
William Maltese's Flicker by William Maltese
My Unborn Child by Orest Stocco
Last Song of the Whales by Four Arrows
Perilous Panacea by Ronald Klueh
Falling but Fulfilled by Zachary M. Oliver
Manifest Intent by Mike Farris
Still Life with Cat and Mouse by Sheila McGraw
Mythical Voyage by Robin Ymer
Hello, Norma Jean by Sue Dolleris
Richer by Jean Blasiar
Charlie No Face by David Seaburn
Number One Bestseller by Brian Morley

Scheduled for Release in early 2011:
Ammon's Horn by G. Amati
In Dire Straits by Jim Currie
In the Himalayan Nights by Anoop Chandola
The Treasure of La Escondida by Carolyn Kingson

Wretched Land by Mila Komarnisky
Chan Kim by Ilan Herman

http://www.savantbooksandpublications.com

CPSIA information can be obtained at www.ICGtesting.com
Printed in the USA
LVOW130240210512

282552LV00005B/15/P